CW01660688

A WINTER RAINBOW

The Diaries of Nelly Sandeman
Compiled and Edited by
Ann Sandeman Tilt

HINDOVER BOOKS

A WINTER RAINBOW
The Diaries of Nelly Sandeman
Compiled and Edited by
Ann Sandeman Tilt

First published by Hindover Books,
50 Hindover Road, Seaford, East Sussex BN25 3NR
England
1998

A catalogue record of this book
is available from The British Library.

Cover Illustrations:
'Roselands' Cottage, Peasemarsh.
Wild Daffodills.
Original watercolours by Nelly Sandeman.

Design and format by StewART

ISBN 0 9533899 0 1

Printed and bound by Antony Rowe Ltd
Bumpers Farm, Chippenham, Wiltshire.

This book is lovingly dedicated to my
Grandmother Nelly (Bell) Sandeman,
to my husband David for his encouragement
and support, also to my dear friend Rita.

AST

"Today I remembered the old Jasmine branch which I had trained round my window, a withered branch, a branch that you would say was dead. Yet inside that branch there drifted, every Spring, the ghosts of a thousand starry blossoms and in its secret channels there was buried a scent of almost intolerable sweetness waiting to be born as soon as the sun should give its blessing."

Nelly Sandeman

A WINTER RAINBOW

CONTENTS

INTRODUCTION

It was during my visit to Victoria, British Columbia, Canada in 1980, to celebrate my Aunt Winnie's eightieth birthday, that I discovered the wicker basket.

The basket had belonged to my Grandma, Nelly Sandeman. Aunt Winnie had sent me down to her cellar to collect some wine and she had mentioned the basket. She suggested that I look inside and if I found anything of interest I could keep it.

On opening the lid I found hundreds of letters, note-books, sketch books, photographs, family memorabilia. My breath was taken away and I spent the rest of that day sifting though the contents of the basket. Nothing was in any order of date but I found within that basket memories of the whole of Nelly's life and that of our forebears. My excitement knew no bounds.

With my Aunt's permission I took some of the basket's precious contents back to England with me and, when I returned to Canada again in 1988, I returned with much more and started to edit Nelly Sandeman's life story.

When Aunt Winnie died in 1994 the wicker basket was sent to me, with the remainder of its treasures. It now has pride of place in my home.

In reading Nelly's papers I came to feel that there was something between us that transcended even the close ties of kinsmanship. I felt a bond that manifested itself in our common love of nature, art and music. Although I was still very young when Nelly died, it gave me great pleasure to read - many years later - an entry in Nelly's diary for April 1938 - a time when I was still a babe in arms.

"Ann is growing fast and appears to like music! Once by chance when I was holding her there was a lovely concert playing on the radio, and baby, that tiny thing of fifteen months listened, yes really listened! As the last lovely notes faded away, she sighed - a long sigh - just as people do at the end of beautiful music. That little thing knew - she was away, her eyes looked dreamy and then that long sigh as the music ceased. I often carry her around the garden and let her smell the roses - she stretches her head towards them, while I hold her hands to prevent her clasping them. To see her inhaling the perfume is magic. I feel she is going to be a lover of beauty."

It has been a great joy and privilege to share Nelly's thoughts and observations and to learn about a life that started its journey half way through Queen Victoria's long reign. I do hope that others derive as much pleasure from these pages as I have enjoyed delving through the treasury of Nelly's basket.

Ann Sandeman Tilt,
Sussex,
Summer, 1998.

ABOUT NELLY SANDEMAN

"Today as I passed down the road, my gaze fastened itself upon the deeply flooded valleys and the hills of Kent beyond. Some spell had drawn my eyes far away over bare woodlands and drowned pastures to a headland jutting out boldly into the levels. As I gazed at this point (which for me always holds a strange fascination) I saw a Winter Rainbow born.

Out of the gray sky spaces, the rainbow colours glimmered faintly, wavered, till the perfect arch, springing on one side from the very foot of the headland and growing brighter as I watched it - framed in like a picture, the beloved land. Quietly it came - impressed itself upon the gray, glowed and suddenly faded, like the Kingdom of Heaven which cometh without observation".

* * * * * * * * * * *

Eleanor Constance (Nelly) Bell was born in 1869 in the City of London. She spent the first few years of her life in the house where she was born, however, the death of her sister Ethel, at the age of 14 months, was blamed on the house drains and so a move was made to the country - near Stoke Newington. Thus began Nelly's lifelong love of the beautiful flowers of the countryside.

Nelly's commune with nature continued on family holidays. At her Papa's parents farm at Sulham, Berkshire or at her Mama's parents' home, The Royal Hotel, Deal.

In 1884, Nelly was sent, with her sister Mabel, to finish her education at a school for young ladies in Karlsruhe, Southern Germany. During her time here she met the man she would love for the rest of her life, a Dragoon Officer, Herr Von Heusch. In those days it was forbidden for a member of the Officer Class to marry an untitled lady - especially one from another country. They wrote to each other during the following years and Von Heusch never married. Upon his death, in 1933, the Von Heusch family returned all Nelly's letters, as he had kept them, neatly tied together with silk.

Following her return to England Nelly studied at The Royal College of Art for a year. Then, in 1890, whilst on holiday in Heidelberg, she met Harry Fraser Sandeman. They were immediately attracted but he was about to leave for Canada to take up cattle ranching. Six years later - much against her family's advice - Nelly followed Harry to Canada and they were married at Strathcona, Alberta, in October 1896.

The first few years were spent farming on the prairies. Nelly lost three babies and she was desperately homesick. In 1899 they moved to the town and Harry started a Real Estate business. A daughter, Eleanor Winifred, was born in 1900 and a son, Roderick, followed four years later. Nelly was able to take solace in her children and in her garden - known locally as "The English Lady's Garden". During this time she also wrote articles for the local newspaper under the pen-name, 'Bill Gubbins'. For many years Harry was completely unaware of the identity of Bill Gubbins.

In 1917 Harry's business failed and the family returned to live in England. At first they stayed with Harry's parents in Ealing, later moving to Greenford. Her son, Roderick went to school at Oxford and in 1920 Eleanor Winifred returned to Canada to marry.

By the mid 1920's Harry and Nelly's marriage failed and Nelly began her time of roaming. She rented rooms and cottages in Sussex and Kent where she painted and wrote about everything she saw in the countryside.

Nelly visited her daughter "Winnie" in Canada several times between 1930 and 1937 and then, in March 1937 a grand-daughter - Ann Primrose - was born to Roderick and his wife Doris.

During the latter years of her life Nelly Sandeman stayed in Somerset, Devon, Shropshire, Surrey as well as her beloved Sussex and Kent. She died in 1943 having suffered a stroke, probably as a result of a wartime bombing. Her last days were spent in a Catholic nursing home where the nuns lovingly cared for her. In fine weather she would be wheeled out to sit beneath an old Mulberry tree, so that her final hours were spent among the things she loved best, the flowers and other gifts of Nature.

Nelly Sandeman is buried at Chiswick.

PART ONE

Nelly Sandeman in 1913

FAMILY AND CHILDHOOD.

CHAPTER ONE
FIRST MEMORIES OF LONDON.

My mind is filled with memories
of those happy childhood days
When the sun seemed
endlessly to shine
And those storm clouds
of my later life
Were far away.

E.S.

I was born on St Patrick's Day 1869, early in the morning, during a snowstorm. I was carried down Giltspur Street to my christening in the old church of St. Sepulchre, not far from Smithfield (Smoothfield) where the Knights rode to Tournaments and close by where the Holy Martyrs suffered by fire, hard by Bartholomew's Hospital.

John Smith of Pocahontas fame lies buried in old St Sepulchre's Church. Papa was a sidesman and freeholder of the Parish when I was born, therefore, the church was specially heated for my christening and two clergymen were present for the ceremony.

A neighbour of ours found time and mood to write a song to greet my arrival. Here are the simple lines he wrote on Good Friday, 26th March 1869.

Nelly Bell

The little birds sing all the day Nelly Bell;
Their songs are delightful to hear,
But no charm have the notes of their musical throats
Like to thy angel voice, Nelly dear.
Many hearts may rejoice at the little bird's voice
(Whether morning or evening it be)
But my Thanksgiving song shall be all the day long
Unto Him who hath giv'n thee to me Nelly dear
Unto Him who hath giv'n thee to me.

The little birds soon fly away Nelly Bell
To the field and the forest afar,
But my own Nelly dear must remain with us here
In our loved happy home, where we are.
And the first little word I will teach thee my bird
(Oh how lovely to hear it from thee!)
Is that one hallow'd name that the Angels proclaim
Of Him who hath giv'n thee to me Nelly dear,
Of Him who hath giv'n thee to me.

J. Playle

* * * * * * * * * * *

In the old city days I had a nurse (from birth), one Sarah Butler, an Irish woman and a widow. With her assistance I used to feed flies with Demerara sugar at our breakfast table.

Sarah was devoted to me, but, as she had a fiery temper, it was thought better that she should leave me when I was four because there was a distinct danger that I was developing the same!

I still have a tender feeling for Sarah Butler, because she loved me and put me first in that, presumably, over-fiery heart. It must have grieved here to part with her nurseling.

Buttercups and daisies
Oh the pretty flowers

Probably from the above two lines, which Sarah taught me, I derived that fervent interest in growing things, which has been a great solace to me throughout my life.

Sarah was allowed to take me about with her. Such, for example, was my visit to Southend, of which, naturally, at that youthful age, I was not fully aware except that it left me with a fear of water which has returned again and again in dreams (or nightmares?)

Wicked looking green water which reached for me, as it were, with evil spurts upward and oh so close to me, although I was carried against a kindly shoulder as we walked up the length of the long pier. She had little idea how frightened a baby she held!

A good forty years later I walked on the same pier at high tide and the sea seemed horribly close to me and my old fears returned.

We lived in our city home until Mama lost her second lovely little girl "Ethel Jeannie" at fourteen months old. I have never been clear as to what carried this beautiful little one away. The illness was called Intermittent Fever and the drains of the old house blamed for it.

A small photograph which we had of her, taken after she fell asleep, showed her long lashes lying on waxen cheeks and her fair hair in rings over the sweet baby brow, one little chubby hand, on the coverlet, held a homely little bunch of fern and flowers and that was baby Ethel, Mother's treasure.

So we moved to Stoke Newington where my sister Mabel was born a year later. Our new house, Ackworth Villa, was near a lovely peaceful village called Stoke Newington and many were the walks we enjoyed across the fields towards Tottenham and Wood Green.

In my great Grandfather Allen's time, gentlemen going home from business in the city used to wait at the corner of what is now Albion Road, Stoke Newington, till there was a sufficient number of them to cross the fields in safety, thus avoiding attacks from footpads.

One of my favourite childhood walks was to follow the New River at Stoke Newington along its flower laden banks. (In summer we picked armfuls of Marsh Marigolds and took them home to Mama).Sometimes we would walk along a path beside the estate of the Clissold family which was called Clissold Park. Through little chinks in the high grey board fence, which separated the Park from Queen Elizabeth's Walk, we caught glimpses of breathtaking beauty. Sheets and sheets of buttercups and emerald grasses.

Before the Prince of Wales (Edward VII) purchased Sandringham there was some talk of him buying the Clissold Estate as a country home.

One little picture my memory retains is of Mama sitting on an old tomb under the lime trees in old St Mary's churchyard (near the Estate), crocheting and smiling at me while I disported myself harmlessly among the tombs, eating gingerbread. The perfume of those lime trees are with me still!

Mama used to talk about a pump near St Clement Dane's old churchyard, which produced the best water in London for the purpose of tea making. The city ladies from far and near would send their maids for the water, which was soft and sparkling.

Bye and bye the authorities discovered that the spring from which the delectable water rose, flowed under the churchyard and its graves, so the pump was closed!

A year after my birth Charles Dickens died and Mama told me many times of Papa going into the Drawing Room and saying "Oh Janie, Dickens is dead". And she replied "Oh no, now we'll never know the end of Edwin Drood!"

Papa had been in the habit of reading Dickens aloud every night while Mama worked at her eyelet hole embroidery.

My brother Harry gave us all great joy with his arrival and I well remember Mama in her Dressing Room, cradling him in her arms and saying "Oh you angelic little thing, how welcome you are in our family!"

I attended a little school a few doors away from home, run by an Irish lady, a Miss Taylor. She was black haired and fair skinned and often wore a dark purple dress with a gold ivy leaf brooch. She had an elderly Grandmama living with her who was the widow of one of Nelson's Admirals and she often used to talk to me when I was sent into the Breakfast Room to practise my scales. She regaled me with tales of her youth. (She lived to be one hundred years.)

I had history lessons with a Miss Penderell, a quiet, gentle young woman. She used to tell me wonderful stories about Charles The Second and I learnt later that the Penderells of Boscobel, who comforted him, were her ancestors.

I remember learning about the Cinque Ports, Hastings, Dover, Romney, Hythe and Sandwich and sometimes Winchelsea and Rye. Whether it was the rhythm that captured me, or even then a shy breath of my future that one day I would dwell in Winchelsea and Rye!

The next school I attended was run by two sisters, the Misses Emily and Harriet Teulon, who were descended from an old Huguenot family.

When starting at the Misses Teulon's school I was determined that my name should be known in full. Why should I always be called "Nelly" when I had such an uncommon name of my own? So, as I was changing my boots to slippers in the place appointed, being asked my name by a teacher I said "Eleanor Constance Bell".

Looking back I know I was exceedingly fortunate in being placed with those kind and good gentlewomen, who were excellent teachers, and whose school room was a warm, happy place where I learnt much. They used to give their pupils outings to the Royal Academy every summer and concerts once a month. From these seeds were sown my lifelong love of art and music.

A friend of Mama gave me my first music lesson - I loved her! Her face was badly pitted by smallpox but her gentle inner nature shone through. When I was a child it was no uncommon thing to meet many people in the street scarred from smallpox, but Annie H was the only person in our immediate circle who was so disfigured.

She gave me one of her childhood treasures - a fairy-tale book translated from the French of Madam D'Aulnoy. It was beautifully illustrated and gave me many hours of pleasure.

Annie married and, alas, moved far away. Many years later we heard that she had been found drowned in the River Thames at Gravesend. I wonder what bitter tragedy and despair drove that dear woman to her desperate end?

Well do I remember walking from The Angel, Islington to the City, hand in hand with Papa and how he always paused to point out a great stone gateway, crossing a side street in Clerkenwell. He, apparently, had a special affection for that old Gateway of St John. (I like to think that I must have gladdened his heart by showing a real interest in it).

So many places Papa showed me, some which Dickens had described in his books, such as The Old Curiosity Shop and Little Nell's home, the Little Nell for whom Papa had a special love and who was my namesake.

Our visits to St Paul's always thrilled me. Seeing the tattered and smoke stained Battle Standards hanging above the tombs of Nelson and Wellington moved me.

Sometimes Papa took me to church on Sunday morning, at the Foundlings Hospital, where the little orphans filled the galleries above us and sang the hymns so sweetly.

When I grew perfect in reading Papa used to encourage me by presents of books that were lovely and of good report, such as John Halifax Gentleman. (Little blind Muriel in that book was a special love of his I noticed, a kindly glow would pass over his face when he spoke of the child).

A head of fine, silky curly hair was one of the first things you noticed about Papa. A very neat figure of a man - upright, soldierly, well proportioned, although not tall as his father was. Papa was one of the early volunteers and also the crack shot of his Battalion, which won him many cups and other silver articles.

Leather still maintained its hold upon us and when my Grandfather Henry Bell retired to Deal, my father succeeded him in the City business, but his heart was not in it and although he was making a thousand pounds a year when I was born, he gave it all up and bought a studio to follow art.

I remember him going to Australia for a year to visit a friend of his youth. (Mama, Mabel and myself, were left behind!)He travelled with another friend who had been to that far country before as guide and companion.

They sailed from London Docks in The Eastern Monarch. Most of his visit was spent on his friend's sheep farm near Melbourne and on leaving for England he was urged to return with his wife and family. I daresay Papa would have liked to but I feel Mama would not have settled so far from her homeland.

My Great Grandparents Bell were Curriers and Tanners. They attended St Andrews Church, Holborn and were buried there. Great Grandma was an Alice Burgess, a Miller's daughter from Aiskew near Bedale, Yorkshire.

My Grandfather, Henry Bell, married Elinor Bassingham, daughter of William Bassingham of Red Cross Street in the City of London. The Bassinghams were Gas Engineers.

My Great Grandfather Bassingham was a churchwarden of Cripplegate Church, where the dust of Milton reposes and Frobisher rests from his voyaging. This was the church were Oliver Cromwell was married. A stained glass window was erected in the church in memory of Great Grandfather and he too was buried in its churchyard.

My Grandmother, Elinor, daughter of William and Mary, had a marvellous singing voice. A great musical authority once happened to hear her singing and went to her father and asked if he would consider having her trained for Grand Opera, which offer he indignantly declined!

My Grandfather, Henry Bell, was twelve years her senior. They lived and brought up a family of four children in the old house where I was born.

When Papa was a small boy his father used to take him to Sadler's Wells to drink the waters. He attended a boarding school on Newington Green in one of those stately old Mansions, long since pulled down. General Fleetwood, son-in-law of Oliver Cromwell once lived in one of those houses.

A great tragedy befell the family when they were driving down Muswell Hill. Something startled the horse and

Papa's Mama, Papa and his eleven year old sister, Nelly, were all thrown out of the trap. Nelly was instantly killed and the others badly shaken and bruised.

Nelly was an adored only daughter and a very loveable girl. Just before they had set out to visit friends, Nelly had looked up at the early evening sky, which was filled with little rosy clouds, and had said to my Papa "How beautiful it looks, I should like to be there".

After the accident, her mother, Elinor, led a very shut in life and gradually faded away and died in her early forties.

When her husband passed away, aged 73, at Walmer, a little tin box was found among his belongings. It contained some lovely gold auburn hair and silk ribbons, carefully wrapped in paper. Papa said it was like uncovering the secrets of a heart.

In after years I remember Papa suddenly rising from the other side of the hearth and snatching the poker away from me as I dreamily stirred the fire, with muttered words "Don't do that, you look just like my mother sitting there!"

My Grandmother's brother, William, had been much attached to her and he too always said I looked like her. In fact, when after not seeing me for five years I paid an unexpected call on his home, his daughters wished to see if he'd still recognise me as a grown up young lady. On his arrival home they presented me saying "Father this is our friend Miss Constance". "How are you Nelly?" he said kindly, much to everyone's amazement as he had last seen me when I was a little schoolgirl with long hair. "I know who you are because you are the image of my poor sister Elinor".

Great Uncle William Bassingham, my father's uncle, was an uncommonly fine looking man with a strong, well featured face, unadorned with any appendages in the shape of moustache and beard. At some period in his later years, finding the inroads of time telling upon his scalp and disliking the thinning of hair, he had his hair completely shaved and wore a black skull cap until his hair grew back thicker and stronger than ever! Not black, but silver white! He was a member of the Court of the Common Council of the City of London and belonged to some other ancient companies.

His wife was a Sussex girl called Sarah Johnson. Her elder sister Elizabeth was his first love but she died very young and some time afterwards he turned to her sister. After their marriage they lived in the city over his place of business (Gas Engineers). Many years after, when their family of two boys and two girls were grown up, they moved to Lordship Park North. He named their new home "Elizabeth House" - it was called No. 92 by the rest of his family.

I spent a lot of time with these Bassinghams from childhood upwards. I remember Great Uncle coming home one evening in a state of indignation. There had been an attempted assassination of Queen Victoria and members of the Corporation of the City of London had journeyed to Windsor to present an address of congratulations to Her Majesty on her escape. Uncle was present and his indignation was caused by the fact that the Queen was separated from them by a red cord, as if she were afraid of contamination!

Great Uncle always had a fire in his breakfast room the year round. No matter how warm the summer was! He expected to find the fire glowing in a cosy, friendly fashion when he returned from the City.

The breakfast room was a delightful room in which to be a little bookworm because Uncle had stacks of bound Punches and Illustrated London News on low bookshelves on each side of the fireplace, which I was allowed to pull out and examine to my heart's content. What cosy, comfortable memories I have of Great Uncle's and Aunt's home. Great Aunt Bassingham was my Godmother and my childhood birthdays were spent with her.

My Mama was born in Haggerston in 1848 and christened at Shoreditch Church. Her first home stood on ground where Shoreditch Station now stands. She remembered an arbour in their garden, covered by Passion Flowers and hearing Nightingales singing there.

She attended a boarding school at Woodford, near Epping. Her mother, Jane Smith a Dry Salter's daughter, died from bronchitis and she remembered being sent home from school, aged nine, to see her mother lying in her coffin.

Mama's father, Robert Allen the second, was left with five young children and within a year he was remarried to a Miss Palmer of Epping whose father kept a school which Robert's son attended. This marriage produced five more children, so in all, my Grandfather had ten!

Great Grandfather Smith, who had greatly loved his daughter Jane, gave his Granddaughter, little Jane (Mama) a fine little piano soon after her Mama's death. She spent holidays with him and was a great comfort to him for the rest of his life.

Watercolours of the Tower of London and Tower Bridge

CHAPTER TWO
FIRST MEMORIES OF KENT

My parents, Henry William Bell and Jane Allen, were married in Upper Deal Church, by the Reverend Griffiths, in May 1867. After a family gathering at The Royal Hotel, they departed for their honeymoon at Tunbridge Wells in a carriage with four horses and Postillions.

My mother, who was then a slender girl of nineteen years (I saw her little wedding bodice with its tiny waist) was grieved at the poor silk her stepmother provided for the wedding gown. That generation were accustomed to silk that stood alone and hers, she said, was like paper.

I have seen a painting of Mama when a young girl, showing she was quite a beauty with long dark hair, blue eyes and a fine clear skin, which she preserved till her last day.

When I was a little girl she had a ballgown which I've never forgotten - it came from the fine old firm Fencott Evans in Upper Street, Islington. It was of an uncommonly lovely shade of lavender blue silk, trimmed with trails of wild convolvulus in pink and white, resting on little clouds of white tulle.

I never see those dainty little flowers blooming without remembering Mama's ballgown!

My Great Grandfather, Robert Allen, was born in 1790. On his mother's side he was descended from a French family. All that Mama knew was that his mother was called Mary. He and his four brothers were orphaned when quite young and were brought up by an Aunt who owned a big cigar business in Spitalfields. (Spitalfields was full of French émigrés and descendants of Huguenots). Robert's brothers were Richard, Charles, Joseph and Thomas.

Joseph and Thomas became very wealthy and lived in Portland Place. They belonged to the Spectacle Maker's Company and used to ride in the Lord Mayor's Show Procession in their splendid scarlet and fur Sheriff's outfits.

After I had been christened Mama received a long telegram from her father, Robert Allen, chiding her because I was not named Jane after his first wife and herself.

His last illness was upon him and his memory failing, yet he remembered, before he died, the needs of his favourite horse and gave instructions that it was to be pensioned off for the rest of its life. But when Grandfather lay dead, his second wife sold it to a Miller and it was condemned to turn round in a circle for its remaining years.

My mother was already married and living in the City when this happened and when she arrived in Deal on her next visit, Grandfather's Groom came to her with tears in his eyes and said "Oh, Miss Janey, Miss Janey, the Master would turn in his grave, if he knew!" There were tears in Mama's eyes as she told me. A grief unforgotten.

According to Mama her father was a very easy going good natured man, very charitable to the poor and very fond of his animals.

There is still the remains of an old soup kitchen in a side street in Deal, a few steps from the sea, that Robert Allen had a great deal to do with, supporting it at a time when the poor of Deal (1840) were suffering. Years ago I met a very old man who still metaphorically smacked his lips when he spoke of "Mr Allen's soup". And another told me "There is no-one like him now, so good to the poor".

As the inhabitants of Deal had never seen a Hansom Cab he had one sent down from London and drove it himself down the middle of the pier so that all might see it.

When Grandfather died all of his ten children took their portion and his widow inherited The Royal Hotel, Deal, which she ran successfully for some years helped by her sister, Betty Palmer.

The second Mrs Robert Allen dies of Dropsy some years after her husband's demise. "Passed away most peacefully" Mama told me.

The Royal Hotel was closed and all the family relics dispersed, no-one knows whither. Save an oil painting of Mrs. Boughton, my Great Great Grandmother, which came into the possession of the youngest of the ten Allen children, Mabel (Mrs James Castle). I saw it hanging in her house at Rochester. It showed a lovely young woman wearing a lace fichu, which was pinned together with that same antique brooch that my Mama gave me, a little oblong brooch containing grey hair, surrounded by a border of pearls.

But what became of Grandma's Crown Derby tea service? No-one knew! I have often wondered where the volumes of The Spectator, the Tatler and Rambler books of Value went.

I remember Aunt Mabel as a girl very clearly. She was about three years older than me. A dear, slender, interesting child, as bright as a little bird. She would take me for walks when I stayed in Deal. Down the little esplanade, northwards we would go, one of her hands clutching my hand with maternal care while, with the other, she steered her doll's perambulator. We always went to a small grocer's shop at the edge of the sea and she bought Garibaldi biscuits, so beloved by us both!

Another memory I have of walks along the esplanade is of great anchors lying on the beach amongst all sorts of junk and flotsam and there were figureheads. This was the remains of the Old Navy Victualling Yard. Victoria Town with its grey terraces and the South Eastern Hotel on the corner, opposite Deal Castle, were built over that romantic spot.

Many of my early Christmases were spent at The Royal Hotel. I remember my first Christmas there very clearly. On our arrival from London we were taken upstairs and I was led into a room out of the dusky passage into bright morning sun shining over the sea and shore and lighting up the quiet figure of my Great Grandma, sitting very erect in a high backed chair, at the left hand side of a long and wide window, overlooking the esplanade and the sea. It was the Nelson Room, the family's private sitting room and an alarmingly big family it seemed to me!

At the head my widowed "half" Grandmama (my mother's stepmother); two youths, her sons, Frank and Harry, of whom I lived in dread as they teased me so! Then my mother's young half sisters, Alice, Jessie and Mabel, all very kind "Aunts" to me and protecting - they made me wear a little warm cape all day, to keep me from the seaside winter cold.

The Hotel was so close to the sea, set down right by the water. On the first floor a verandah ran the whole width of the Hotel overlooking the sea and the waves came splashing over a low wall on the beach in rough weather, flinging their spray onto the windows, to my mingled horror and delight. It was bleak and cold, my relations thought, for a little delicate city child, subject to croup, therefore the little warm cape. But when it came that I was not allowed to wear my black velvet frock trimmed with white swansdown, on the occasion of the Grand Christmas Party, I felt rebellious indeed and not even allowed to wear the rose-pink frock with its black velvet ribbon trimmings. No I must not change my frock, I must keep on the little everyday blue dress and it was *not at all* like a party frock!

I remember feeling like a little dingy sparrow might among fine plumaged birds, for it was a very grand Christmas Party indeed. All the young people of Deal seemed to be gathered together. Holly and Mistletoe everywhere and great glowing fires in all the rooms. The merry making and the joyous laughter remains with me yet.

Somehow I cannot remember Great Grandmother Allen ever talking to me. She seemed apart, just a dignified presence of whom I was in awe. Considering that she was then about ninety years old she must have been tired and bewildered surrounded by such a big lively family.

She used to sleep in a room at the side of the house, which my mother used to share with her when young. The one window looked out onto a little cobble paved courtyard, one of those little courts or alleys which ran from Beach Street to the shore.

She was born in 1782 - Jane Boughton. She was orphaned very young but had four brothers who all became clergymen of the Church of England. These four men were engaged to four sisters. Three of the couples married but, sadly, the fourth sister died. Jane passed most of her childhood living with relations, the Green family, who lived in great state in an old mansion at Streatham. One of her cousins was married to Sir Kingsmill Key, twice Lord Mayor of London.

The Greens owned a Shipping Company "The Stuarts and John Company", which had been theirs since Tudor times and was reputed to be the oldest of its kind in the world, with its splendid Clippers rushing homewards with their cargo of tea.

My Mama recollected her Grandmother telling her many amusing stories and her favourite one was about the Hall in the Streatham Mansion, where the footmen, before going out with the carriage, would pop their heads (or wigs through the window of a little powder closet to receive a dusting of powder. "It was a little window rather like a ticket office" said Mama.

Great Grandma lived with her relations until her first marriage to Thomas Milo. (The Milo's were a well known family in the City). They had three children, Thomas, Theophilus and Jane.

A few years after her marriage she had a remarkable dream. She dreamed of a winning number in a lottery. The next day she applied for that number ticket and it won!

After her husband died she sold his Tobacco Business and lived quietly with her young children until she met and married Robert Allen. They had one son, Robert, the second, and resided in the City until Great Grandfather retired and they went to live in the country at Wood Green. After his death, his wife went to live with their son Robert at The Royal Hotel, Deal, which she had helped him buy some years before.

Great Grandma's other children all led interesting lives. Thomas ran and owned a Club in The Strand, which Edward VII, as Prince of Wales, frequented. He was a talented artist and exhibited at the Royal Academy.

Theophilus had a business in the City. He married a Laura Williams, a tall queenly girl.

Jane married William Fradeley, a City Stockbroker. Their eldest son, John, became Manager and Director of the Union Bank of Scotland in Cornhill. He was always kind enough to invite us to the Bank to witness the procession of the Lord Mayor's Show.

For some years we spent Christmas with John and his family in their house at Brondesbury. A gallery ran all round the upper floor, very impressive to me as a youngster and splendid for games.

This keeping Christmas together continued until John, the eldest son, Mabel and I went our different ways to school in Germany. John attended a celebrated Moravian school on the Rhine.

Every summer Mama and Papa took Mabel, Harry and I to stay at Deal for Regatta week. The whole families of Allen and Bell, from the oldest to the youngest were there and much fun and laughter was enjoyed. The Regatta took place between The Royal Hotel and the pier and we would sit on the Hotel verandah to watch the races.

After our week in Deal we moved on to Kingsdown where my Grandfather Bell rented Minor Cottage for a month each year. Kingsdown was then a very quiet little fishing village lying due south of Walmer, with a beach situated beneath chalk cliffs and a steep, winding street. The church was built in 1850 with money endowed by a local resident, William Curling.

Mama used to play the harmonium in the church. On hot summer afternoons I would frequently accompany her. "Oh rest in the Lord, wait patiently for him" came welling forth from the open church door where Mama sat playing, surrounded by memorials to departed Curlings, whilst I, outside, was gathering wild flowers and laying them on the graves which had no headstone, on the cold, cheerless north side of the church.

"Oh rest in the Lord, wait patiently for him and he shall give thee thy heart's desire"

Such a wave of comfort and consolation swept over me while those fingers of my mother wove out that lovely music inside the church.

Nightingales in the season sang in the little copse through which a path wound from the vicarage and upper village.

Two inns supplied the wants of the villagers, mostly fishermen, and their families. The Victory Inn and The Rising Sun.

One of Nelly's early watercolours from Kingsdown

Sometimes I would sit on the cliff near the church, dangling my legs over the edge, watching the scenes below me of the comings and goings of those who dwelt there. One street and a half was situated on the shingle and ran down to the sea.

The view as I sat there drew my young eyes over to Pegwell Bay to the north and Ramsgate, where the sea was the colour of grey pearl, softly fading into distance.

One day one of the fishermen's wives told me about the wreck of a Great East Indiaman and the poor young man who lost his bride and was saved himself. He wandered up and down the beach, crazed with grief, mad with misery all day long.

One of our playmates was a little fair haired boy who wore a long trousered sailor suit and straw hat. Our Mamas sat together on the beach while we children played happily together on that quiet shore and hunted for cowries (little oval shells) which were plentiful there. That little boy grew up to be "Hassal" a well known illustrator. Many of his illustrations bear vivid evidence to his early years spent in and around Kingsdown.

Mabel and I went as boarders to a school in Deal, Carter House, for a year before going to Germany. Carter House overlooked the sea and was an interesting old place, built in an "L" shape.

Our big bedroom, which we shared with the two daughters of the house, looked out into Middle Street which, two hundred years ago, was the quality street of Deal, inhabited by the families of seafaring Admirals and other officers. For some time it degenerated exceedingly.

Now, however, many of the old houses are being rediscovered and their long hidden beauty revealed, unsuspected oak panelling and even an Adam staircase. The sea views were always most interesting, with sailing vessels sheltering in the Downs while waiting for a favourable wind.

Papa would come down to see us and stay with his father at Castle Street, Walmer, where we were invited to tea, in which Sydney Ord's Farmhouse Jam and Plumcake always figured. Never were such jams as Sydney Ord's, whoever he was, one feels like blessing his jammy soul - wherever it rests!

I remember the deep cool moss grown well in Grandpa Bell's garden, a lovely olde worlde garden with a back gate opening onto a great expanse of fields and green downland. Such lovely velvety Polyanthuses grew in his garden; it was there that I first fell in love with them.

Papa sometimes took us to stay with friends of his at Herne Bay, then a dear little sunny place. The road from the station at once admitted us to its treasures - its footpaths wreathed with pink and white convolvulus flourishing, as they always did, amidst the white dust of the roadside. That quiet country road led us quickly to the seashore by the Tamarisk Hedges. Happy memories indeed.

The Isle of Sheppey looming in the estuary westward, an enchanted Isle to me, and the sun slipping down behind the sea, the most magical thing of all!

Oh the beauty of our rambles to Reculver. First through the sweet smelling bean fields, then up through the cornfields on the cliffs and, below, a shimmering summer sea.

Then there were the happy evenings when Papa would drive us inland to the village of Herne in his friend's trap with a lovely white pony pulling us, returning to bed when the first stars appeared.

The ways of old
The ways of youth
Oh these I'll treat no more!
Anon.

PART TWO

GERMANY.

CHAPTER THREE
UNFORGETTABLE EXPERIENCES

I am just writing down things as they occur to my mind. Although what I really wish to do (and how impossible it seems now) is to recreate for you that loveliness which I found waiting for me in Southern Germany when I was a girl of sixteen in 1884.

No wonder Papa had said, as he saw us off at Liverpool Street Station, "Now you are going to have experiences you'll never forget."

Anyway, here are my memories of those far off days, all mixed up in a pot pourri.

Our journey from London to Karlsruhe in April 1884 was an interesting one, via Rotterdam, Brussels, Waterloo, Metz, Nancy and Strasbourg. I clearly remember the blue Ardennes and the little white crucifixes at the roadsides. Brussels was a city of fine buildings, but rather too noisy for my liking!

Our stay in Metz was enjoyable. There was music playing in the courtyard of our hotel. We walked one morning on the fortifications of the old wall and visited the lovely cathedral where we met our first German soldiers - a regiment returning from exercises with their kindly smiling young officers bowing to us. No doubt we were immediately recognised as foreigners. Our pretty young mama, dressed in claret coloured velvet, and Mabel and me in wine coloured cloth coats, with shoulder capes trimmed with marabou. Doubtless we three felt shy at finding ourselves the sole target of glances from a regiment of soldiers.

Not many people from England went to Metz in those days but Papa had mapped out this route as the most interesting one, through the battlefields of the Franco-Prussian war (1870 - 1871). Our train journey continued to Nancy and Strasbourg. We crossed the Rhine at Appenweier into beautiful Baden.

The Black Forest looked as dark as a thundercloud as we approached it - how truly named.

At first we saw waterfalls coursing down the mountains, an added delight to young eyes which had never seen mountains before. As the day went on, the mountains to our right began to fall away in height and distance as we neared Karlsruhe until they remained as a background of high hills to our first view of the town.

On leaving the train we had some trouble to get ourselves understood. Bismarckstrasse was, of course, instantly recognised by the driver of our cab, but the number he could not understand spoken in English. He seemed to be highly amused however and mounting his box he soon drove us through the town to Bismarckstrasse and then deposited us at the door of the Von Gemmingems', still smiling broadly!

A most indignant maid of the superior order (dressed like, and with the manners of, a stage maid) dismissed us and the coachman. She informed us that there was a school for English ladies further along the street. The coachman cheerfully ushered us back into the coach and, this time with better success, deposited us and our luggage at our destination, 71 Bismarckstrasse, where we received a more kindly welcome.

Some little sound upstairs made me raise my eyes as we entered the hall and I saw one or two girls leaning over the banisters; they rushed back into their schoolroom to announce that the new girls had arrived.

Mama stayed for some weeks at the Hotel Germania, so we were not plunged unaccompanied into our strange surroundings!

When Mama was returning to England and leaving us alone in a strange land, she emptied our her purse between Mabel and me that evening in her room in the Hotel Germania. She had plenty, she said, to see her through. “But you never know!” said I, with the wisdom of my fifteen years. Mabel and I looked at each other and, when Mama was not observing us, we put all she had given us quietly back into her purse and felt comforted.

As things turned out she badly needed that money owing to some mishap connected with the trains. She missed her connection somewhere and had to put up for the night in some odd place - poor little Mama, in the dark among strangers, unable to speak a word of their tongue, imagine it!

However, on she went the next day and found herself in Antwerp and on to the boat, vastly to her relief I’m sure. She was quite at the end of her resources, in spite of the coins we had returned to her purse, so she had no breakfast and no money to give her stewardess the next morning. Mama asked the women for her address so that she might forward to her the tip which she naturally felt was owing.

The school was owned and run by Frau Nickles. I always remember her extreme neatness of habit (which, indeed, all German ladies followed) and the little silken soft rings of flaxen curls at the nape of her neck, like silkworm silk fresh wound from the cocoon. She gave us a real home, good care, excellent food and lovely surroundings but, somehow or other, these things were recognised too late by me and there was always an antagonism, or so I then felt, between us.

We were returning from a walk one day when we came across an officer of Dragoons (whom I later learned was Herr Von Heusch), not far from our garden gate. He stopped but a moment as we passed, said "Guten Morgen", saluted and passed on. Frau Nickles was standing on the balcony, outside her study window, watching us. Indoors she took me into her study and spoke, as I see now, very gravely and wisely, but not altogether kindly. She said it was quite out of place that an officer of noble birth and of a distinguished regiment, should recognise and salute a little, middle class, English schoolgirl and, with some subtlety she showed me the gulf which lay between that little English girl and an officer of the German Army who could only marry a lady of rank and fortune, as was his right.

I was bewildered! It appeared that our friend had called, at his mother's wish, on the children of her English acquaintance, our Mama, and the chocolates he bought for us were either returned to him or confiscated. Well, little innocent silky curls not withstanding, Frau Nickles certainly was antagonistic.

One day she called me into her study and forbade me to curl my fringe. "You look like a lion with it curled" she said (remarkable statement) - but I reflected that, after all, the lion was the King of the beasts!

Another time, when we were all descending the stairs together, attended by one French and two German governesses, preparing to set off for a walk, Frau Nickles, coming out of her room, singled me out from my companions and sent me upstairs to "take off *that*", pointing to my dress improver - a quite modest one, by the way, and in no sense different to those worn by the older girls. (I was then sixteen). Blushing and indignant I ascended the stairs to my room, took off the offending article and joined my waiting companions - you can imagine how I felt!

"You will be led but you won't be driven" said Mademoiselle Landrey once to me. The teachers were dear women, never a satirical or unkind word from them, just kind looks, understanding words and sometimes amused smiles.

Frau Nickles had three children, Edward, Anna and Otto. Edward I don't remember much of - a heavily built, stout, fair fellow, with rather a rugged face. He was a divinity student and, judging by his friends, a very good sort.

Anna was tall and very classic looking. She was very kind and gentle and her close set, rather small, greenish eyes never looked at us but in mild kindness and affection. In

"Fur Meine Mutter Liebe" Sept. 9th 1884

the big schoolroom a large bust of Caesar presided over the scene and there was a strong family likeness between Caesar and Anna I always thought - a marked resemblance.

Little Otto was a brother to us, albeit a very teasing and tormenting one! He was about twelve, very plain and delicate looking but his whimsical face was lit up for me always by his innate loveableness (little friend of all the world). It was Otto who caused me to forsake the old spelling of my name - viz. Nelly. I see his sly look now when he would make a rhyme out of my full name, knowing how *shocked* I was! So I altered it to Nellie and never felt at home with it afterwards!

Once, disobeying a rule by bringing an inkpot downstairs, it fell over the banisters and splashed the stone steps leading to the hall below. I was terrified and, of course, Frau Nickles was soon on the scene in her inimitable, silent manner, as of a ghost appearing. She said nothing but she looked at me with a withering look as she passed. Little Otto and Mabel, who were with me, endeavoured to wipe away the damage, Otto whispering "Never mind Nellie, I'll help you". Dear little, kind Otto, but we didn't keep him long, he died a few months later. We were called into the darkened salon to see that still marble face and to kiss his brow in a last farewell. We were kept very ignorant concerning his illness, pneumonia, and his death was a great shock to us.

As I kissed him I knew instantly that Otto was not there. The butterfly had flown and left behind its empty shell, but that knowledge did not stem my tears. I had never known death face to face before and it was bitter.

What a dear, kindly set of girls were my companions at 71 Bismarckstrasse. I cannot remember a single quarrel or unpleasantness between us but then I cannot either remember a day of rain or storm during this period but there **must** have been grey days. My memory holds only lovely weather. For me the sun always shone and it was glorious weather!

My companions came from far and wide, Florrie Body from Tiverton, Devon, flaxen haired and plain of face but with the most charming manners and the kindest heart.

Mary Douglass of Tilquhillie, a little impish, fairy of a girl who instantly made a great friend of my sister, Mabel. Fine, earnest deep grey eyes, dark lashed with an abundance of flaxen gold hair, which she wore in a heavy plait, and very fair skin. She always wore a curious ring which her Grandfather, the Laird of Tilquhillie, had had made for her - a great carbuncle surmounted by the crest of the Douglasses. Mary later married Edward Fairburn of Canterbury.

Clara Rotharmel, a kindly girl with the nutcracker face of an old woman. Her mother was dead and her father an old man. From her I first heard that pretty German word of endearment "Herzblattchen" (my heart's little green leaf, or little green leaf of my heart).

Louisa Tanzbein - dance leg we called her because she was always pirouetting. A fair, thin, inoffensive creature.

Julie Hegi from Neuchâtel, Switzerland, who had very fine eyes, usually wearing an intensely proud and self possessed expression.

Eva Baker from Twickenham, an extremely handsome girl with wonderful, long, thick wavy dark chestnut hair, growing gradually fairer till it reached a rich gold at the ends of her plait. A beautiful profile, but a noticeably hard chin and firm mouth. She afterwards became a governess to the De Lesseps family in Paris.

Jessie Robertson was absolutely brim full of fun, humour and kindness. I never saw her out of temper. She had twinkling soft brown eyes, most irresistible, a lot of wavy brown hair worn in a great heavy pleat that needed no ribbon as her hair curled beautifully at the ends.

It was the time of dress improvers and cushions. Jessie wore a crimson satin cushion of which we got occasional peeps owing to the fashion of dress fastenings in those days! Two or three years later, in England, when Mabel was in a strange church, she unexpectedly saw Jessie sitting in front of her and looked involuntarily to see if Jessie's cushion was showing!

Other names that come to my mind are Emily Deichman, Clara Friese and a lovely Irish girl called Annie who was truly lovely, the beauty and queen of us all. A heart shaped face with the pink and pearl of a wild rose, eyes of greeny blue, an adorable little straight nose which matched a sweet, but most wilful, mouth, a delightful little plump rounded figure and milk white neck and hands - all crowned by her pretty light brown hair, which she wore in a mass of curls. Our eyes always sought and found each others - tear filled but unashamed - when wonderful music was played. All dear friends and others who were there with me, pass on in my mind now as shadows - beloved shadows.

Our teachers were good and kind to us and the ones I remember with affection are Joanna Livingstone from Kirkcaldy. Such blue eyes! She was most excellently educated in Scotland and instructed Mabel and me (the youngest in the school) in English, particularly punctuation, and very beautiful English it was! Also she gave us our earliest lessons in the German language but, after three months of the most excellent tuition, she returned home. The impression she made has never faded.

Fraulein Helbeck, so patient and yet so aristocratic - so sweet and kindly and understanding in all her ways and yet so dearly, dearly human! We used to consider her elderly - she was probably in her early thirties. She had rather thin, wavy hair of a brown that matched her clear hazel eyes. She wore it parted in the middle and drawn waving back and knotted simply, a style that suited her perfectly but which, to the eyes of young girls, would have looked old fashioned in the days of ugly frizzes and hair dragged up straight, revealing the ears - which prevailed in England in the 1880's. I rather fancied that she was going to be married on leaving at the end of one term, but she was too reserved to give much information about her doings. We knew she came from a fine family and I suspect that Von might easily have preceded the Helbeck (clear stream or brook). Like so many other things, I bitterly regret that I did not avail myself of the privilege she gave me of writing to her and so lost sight of her.

Our professor of French Literature was a man of stern face and voice, who never smiled. He frightened me but, on reflection, I think he was in possession of a sense of humour! Voltaire was his hero and he taught me to love words. I think he came from Brittany.

We were taught Ballet by the Grand Ducal Dancing Master and Music by Herr Kalliwoda, the last living pupil of Mendelssohn. Johnfields Nocturne was the first music given to me to learn and play. This nocturne stirred within me and I've always loved it and when I play it now it takes me back to those happy days.

Our school was situated on the edge of the west side of Karlsruhe. Bismarckstrasse opened into Westenstrasse and the Forest. In Bismarckstrasse dwelt the Head of the Army with sentries at his gate.

Worthstrasse was a turning out of Bismarckstrasse, with a vista of forest at the end. I remember it for its glorious tints of Virginia Creeper which covered the houses' balconies against a background of intensely blue sky.

The main square was situated in the middle of the town with streets spreading fanwise from it. In the centre of this square rose a stone pyramid in which the heart of Carl Markgraf of Baden, founder of the town, reposed, in the midst of his faithful people.

There, surrounding the pyramid, you found old country women sitting by their little stalls, under the shelter of their big coloured umbrellas, selling their simple wares of apples, eggs, butter, cheese, boiled chestnuts, etc. The Ladies of the Court would sally forth early accompanied by their cooks carrying capacious baskets to buy food.

There was a fairytale castle and park, called the Fasanien Garter (The Pheasant Preserve). This park was wild and beautiful and only to be entered by special permission from the Grand Duke, which Frau Nickles never failed to obtain.

Sometimes, in my mind, I catch sight of the silver spray of the fountain, the Castle Gardens (Schlossgarten) and hear the music played by the Military Band which seemed to accompany us from morning to night. Hidden under the trees they played soft melodies and rousing marches. From our balcony the gleam of their instruments could be glimpsed through the foliage.

The Black Dragoons were stationed near the Castle. Theirs was a Vornchmes Regiment, otherwise a crack Regiment. They rode past our school daily and we would rush on to the balconies to watch them pass. Herr Von Heusch asked to be permitted to teach both Mabel and me to ride. We were to attend the Riding School of the Black Dragoons at their barracks but, alas, no advantage was taken of this opportunity as Mama felt unable to accept the invitation. (Daughters and wives of the Regiment were accustomed to ride there). I did try to persuade Mama but to no avail. There was an idea current at the time that I should have a good seat and look well on horseback! Herr Von Heusch also seemed anxious to teach me shooting (revolver practise) but that too was vetoed!

We were introduced to Frei-Herr Ludwig Von Ungern-Sternberg of the Grenadier Guards. He struck me as rather a supercilious gentleman. He made me wince once or twice with sarcasm that did no credit to his noble birth. I didn't fancy his extreme fairness of colouring - he lacked that golden brown I so admired! He was present to us mainly, I believe, because he had an English mother. Certainly his languid utterances in our language proved that English was indeed his mother tongue. He used to thoroughly enjoy "Tit-bits" and we used to occasionally put bundles of that green covered magazine through his open window on the ground floor of a house in the Kaisenstrasse.

I have one memory of him that I like to remember. Mama, Mabel and I were taking the lonely path around the lake in the Stadt-garter one summer evening - away from the music and friendly chatter of people at little tables under the trees, when we met, to our surprise, Herr Von Ungern-Sternberg moping alone by the shores of the lake. Really unlike his usual superior self, he told us that he was sure that France and Germany would be at war soon and it was worrying him. Considering his unimportant audience of three it was not worth his while to be anything but sincere. He really was downhearted and had dropped that languid superior manner and become quite human! He shed a very real and depressing influence on us and yet I liked him for the first time. What breath of forewarning reached him that summer night in Karlsruhe so very long ago?

He fell in Austria during the Great War.

There was a Conditorei in the Kaiserstrasse in Karlsruhe where they had boat shaped nut cakes of such incredible richness and depth that, after eating two at a sitting, I could never be prevailed upon to touch another. There were delicious tartlets containing green grapes and whipped cream and, for sweets, we loved especially those little green "gooseberries" with their sweet, acid flavour. This shop was on the right hand side of the Kaiserstrasse, looking down towards the Black Forest. There we spent most of our Saturday pocket money - save what we put by for birthday presents for each other and for our soap, gloves and stamps.

One shop in Zirkel Strasse had a big glass jar, with a little wooden ladder in it, in which lived two grass green frogs. According to the weather, they were up or down the ladder and they caused us much mild excitement as we walked by.

Then there were the small mirrors outside people's windows in all the streets of the town. This, to us, was an amazing custom, used to the prim regularity of London windows in the 80's. The reason for the mirrors was that the foot passengers and passing traffic could be observed from the safe vantage of the house within, without any vulgar craning of head or neck! I often thought that an invalid might have their tedium greatly relieved by catching a glimpse of the outside world.

Herr Von Heusche dwelt in Zirkel Strasse for a while, over a baker's shop not far from the Castle. One day he showed us his tame canary which hopped up and down his arm and pecked at his golden up-twisted moustache.

The baker's wife looked askance at us, rather grimly, when we called and asked for the Herr Lieutenant. We were only two young girls returning books that had been lent and we never dreamt a chaperone was necessary, but apparently the baker's wife thought it was! It was our last visit there alone!

Every Saturday evening, prettily attired, we entered the Salon for music, games, dancing and charades. Frau Nickles allowed Edward, Anna and Otto to invite their friends too and we really had some excellent entertainment, especially from Edward's friends who were all very gifted young men and added much to our pleasure, although, as far as I remember, none of them touched our English hearts in the slightest degree (and I expect Edward had had his orders!) I do remember one of those proper young men fixing his eyes on a pair of new patent leather court shoes, just out from England, that I was wearing. I looked down myself to see the cause of his interest and I realised it was my new shoes which did look absurdly tiny, peeping out from my long skirts. I withdrew them immediately - this would have been called "vanity" in that generation, but I thought it merely "funny". German feet were more substantial!

I always chose a low seat in a corner from whence I could survey the company quietly, which I found a feast in itself.

Frau Nickles sat in state and dignity, knitting and leading the games from her armchair. After Professor Nickles died she must have had hard times with the school to run and three children to bring up and educate. I saw long ago that she was all too often misunderstood by most of us and we sometimes looked upon her as our natural enemy. If only we could have hugged her once in a while! But she was a very dignified woman and discipline must always be maintained.

I remember the services held by an English chaplain, a very tall, frail, gaunt, auburn haired man, dying by inches from consumption, in an upper room near the West End Gate. We English had no church of our own so the room was used instead.

How green were the horse chestnuts glimpsed through the open windows and how refreshing the cool breeze blowing upon us. Prayers were always said for our Queen and for the Grand Duke of Baden and the Hereditary Grand Duke, over which latter title the poor chaplain invariably stumbled.

On high days and holidays we attended services in the Castle Chapel. Mabel and I wore our "best" dresses of apricot crêpe de laine trimmed with lace. I nicknamed the clergyman "Herr Rook" because in his black surplice he reminded me of that bird! His sermons were always long. How gladly we chanted the threefold amen at the end and made our exit to the sunlight. Listening to his sermons I always felt that I was part of an audience from the time the door in the upper wall popped open like a cuckoo clock door and out came Herr Rook with his little book. He was like a great Shakespearean actor.

How different a world it was to the North London suburb I was used to, with its stifling respectability.

CHAPTER FOUR
PARADISE FOR A WHILE

We were taken to philharmonic concerts in the "Museums Hall". We girls had nicknames in plenty for some of the performers who we used to watch so frequently on the platform before us - we were always well up in front. I remember the Pea or Pumpkin, one of the singers, a middle aged woman with scant hair and that very tightly twisted up into a little round knot on the very top of her head, which, with the big broad colourless face underneath, bore out the resemblance.

We attended the first performance of Wagner's Siegfried at the Court Theatre with Herr Felix Mottl conducting. Frau Cosima Wagner and her family sat in the Distinguished Strangers box which jutted out squarely from the centre of what we would call the Dress Circle. It was a notable occasion, Frau Wagner having undertaken the long journey to Karlsruhe in order to be present for this momentous performance. We were sitting quite close, not far from her in the Circle, and naturally regarded her with lively interest shared, I am sure, with everyone in the Theatre. I remember finding her, in my youthful eyes, a very ordinary, elderly, quiet woman - Frau Wagner, daughter of Liszt and widow of the great Wagner.

Liszt, I deeply regret to say, I missed seeing and hearing when he was in Karlsruhe. All the other girls went but I had a headache and begged off. I was allowed to stay at School, rather to my surprise, but expect my ticket was fully utilised and probably welcomed by the powers that were!

The officers of the four Regiments quartered in Karlsruhe always occupied the first two rows of the stalls in the Court Theatre, making a fine show themselves in their uniforms when, at the interval, they stood with their backs to the stage and surveyed the audience upstairs and down, very thoroughly, through their opera glasses, lingering where they found interest most unblushingly.

It was told in Karlsruhe that the Grand Ducal Ballet girls were all "old women" and that the Grand Duchess herself had seen to that matter, but I can remember Fraulein Fritsch of the Court Theatre Opera singing at a concert "Roslein, Roslein, Roslein soth Roslein auf der Heiden". I can see her pretty, starry eyes up-raised to show their starriness, while she sang to us. Dear little lovely creature, a slender girl, so unlike, in build or countenance, our other magnificent Prima Donnas. She was perfect as the heroine of Victor Von Scheffel's Operetta "The Trompeter Von Säckingen". Her cruel father, the Noble Count, had just banished, from his Castle of Säckingen in Baden, his Castle Trompeter for daring to ask for the hand of his motherless daughter. It is nightfall and the lovers part! The Trompeter, in moving fashion, is seen afar singing his song (Yang Werner's Abscheed). Then, sounding his last farewell, you hear the notes of his trumpet dying away in the distance. "Father" she cries, and to this day I wonder how Fraulein Fritsch managed, in that one word, to convey the appeal, the reproach and the heartbreak. No, I couldn't help it, the tears would rush to my eyes!

One of our favourite walks in springtime was to Appen-Mühle, a village some little distance from Karlsruhe. We delighted in the sandy banks of a winding stream which turned the mill wheel. There we gathered wood anemones and marsh marigolds while we rambled in the copse beside the water.

Appen-Mühle, as I remember it, was a typical south German village, complete with geese and a goose girl. The mill by the stream and the queer little church tower were all just as you see illustrated in a Grimm Fairytale book. I was very fond of the little place.

We also loved to walk in the Forest with its smooth, even paths opening into wide allies (rides). The thick moss, the ferns and the multi-coloured fungi, which we would take home to paint. So novel to us were the forms and colours.

In summer we would plunge deep into the cool green recesses looking for strawberries which grew wild there. The mingled fragrances of the strawberries, pine trees and a hundred other delicious perfumes are impossible to describe.

Once, when we were strawberry picking, we were startled by Herr Von Heusch and some other Dragoons. They rode up behind us and so frightened me that I cried out. A moment before there had been no-one in sight! They plunged deep into the rough forest and I feared for their heads among the branches!

Violets, blue and white, scattered over the graves in the old churchyard at the edge of the town. This was the church of the Brothers Minor Franciscan Order, but we knew it only by the name of the Old Church Yard, and no other, in our time.

Surrounded by high buildings now, it was *then* canopied by the sky alone and there was an air of wistful musing sweetness about those old graves of the nobility of bygone days, scattered over with violets blue and white. Which reminds me of the beautiful German custom of dressing the graves with flowers on All Souls' Day, when everyone went to the cemetery beyond the town. *Throngs* of people of all classes and ages carrying wreaths and flowers to deck the resting places of their beloved. You would meet those you knew and those you didn't know, a devout and filial pilgrimage.

At Christmas tiny trees were put on the graves and many lit with candles in remembrance.

We had many excursions to interesting places around Karlsruhe. Often in summer we would take a train early in the morning to Baden-Baden - what delightful breaks in our work were these excursions. Our journey took us via the Fortress of Rastätt, which was, as it were, the curtain going up before a play and then, in a few minutes, it seemed we were plunging into the recess of the Black Forest where Baden-Baden lay and a whole day of perfect beauty was before us.

Once we visited the Castle and, in the absence of the Grand-ducal family, were shown over their private apartments, having been furnished with big felt slippers to wear over our shoes to prevent spoiling the beautiful polished parquet floors.

I can still remember the enchanting view over the valley from one of the sitting rooms, or boudoirs, and a painting in oils of wild roses which stood on an easel near the window, executed by Princess Victoria of Baden, who was wife of the Crown Prince of Sweden. "Poor Princess Victoria" said Frau Nickles to me with a compassionate sigh, "that she must live in the cold north, so far away from her beloved Baden".

As we went wandering up the hillsides we found high hedges of Syringa in blossom and a little spring of sparkling water where we all tried out our newly purchased little drinking cups. Once, on a ramble, we found an old graveyard attached to a Convent and there was a grave of a nun who had been blind. She had died years and years before, almost a century perhaps, and there on her tombstone were these words: 'Sie sah wieden' (She saw again).

We had so many happy days wandering in and around Baden-Baden and in the evenings, after hours of bliss and interesting happenings, we once more entrained for our residing town.

One day we visited Durlach, which is set on the high foothills of the Black Forest. I climbed up to the old Roman Watch Tower - Oh, the light, the colour, the mellow distances, each fading into each other, the utter romance of it all is indescribable. If ever a creature reached Paradise for a space that day, it was I. "Never mind," thought I, "if I'm blind when I die, I was in Paradise for a while!"

So many places visited, so many happy hours spent seeing new places. The summer evenings returning to Karlsruhe from these excursions over the country roads, singing aloud to our hearts content.

I remember, with delight, the skating holiday when the ice first became firm (or so we thought!) The falling in of all the girls when it cracked and our rescue, followed by a mournful and dripping procession down the Westenstrasse, followed by little jeering boys hooting at us. The punishment which followed and Frau Nickles writing on the notice-board "Fresh water Backfische to be obtained at 71 Bismarckstrasse!" Backfische being the German term for schoolgirl or flapper!

One afternoon we followed the lovely little river, which flows through Baden Baden - we had no river in Karlsruhe. We found a pretty little cafe under the mountain, with tables covered by the most beautifully embroidered tablecloths and shaded from the sun by large trees. Black Forest girls, black haired with deep blue eyes, waited upon us, smiling. Attired in their Black Forest costumes, their little black velvet bodices bespread with silver filigree chains and ornaments and their black ribbon head-dresses, they served us with iced cakes covered with little wild strawberries, sweet and well flavoured.

During another outing to Baden-Baden we climbed a hilly path which led us to an old ruined castle. It was a day of showers and the valley below was veiled with mist and clouds floated by. The sound of the wind in the surrounding pine trees mingled with the music of harps which were being played within the ruins. The wind and music wove themselves together in my mind and, to this day, whenever I hear harps, I remember that scene.

Later, we were taken down into the dungeons, which were awesome. Oh the thickness of their great doors, which our guide slowly swung shut when we were in one of the cells. A ghastly sense of hopelessness fell upon me in the darkness.

Sometimes we were taken on evening trips to Maxau on the Rhine to bathe. We would rush helter skelter to our bathing cabinets to change, such a happy throng we were! Large baskets of food always accompanied us with raspberry cordial to drink.

We once met the Grand Duke and Grand Duchess walking in the Westenstrasse, apparently unattended. We were on our way back to school from a long country ramble, when we perceived an elderly lady and gentleman approaching us. We took them to be just an officer and his wife, so unassuming were they. As they reached us they looked at us almost individually - we were walking in a crocodile - and smiled benevolently. One of our teachers suddenly recognised them and said in a voice filled with horror "They were the Grand Duke and Duchess and we never bowed!!" But *I'm* sure they understood!

It was certainly surprising to us English girls to meet Royalty in the street. Just imagine meeting Queen Victoria and one of the Princes walking unattended in Pall Mall!

I saw the Grand Duke driving through the woods one summer evening with his cousin, Max of Baden. I was with some of my friends and teachers sketching. We were sitting in our favourite trees which bordered the track. A voice called up to us in our chosen tree seats, "I hope you are all enjoying yourselves up there". Such a jolly, rollicking voice it was. It belonged to Max of Baden, who later became Grand Duke Max and who so finely and courageously condemned many of his country's actions in the War of 1914 - 18.

Then there were the gala days, such as the Kaiser's birthday (the old Emperor William I). He was literally worshipped by his subjects - such colour, such verve!

We were all shepherded to the Stadt Kirche and seated up in the great gallery that ran round three sides of the church. From there we looked down on the massed soldiers and officers beneath. Such music and blaring of trumpets in the great square outside when the Regiments marched past in review. The officers waving their swords and gracefully skipping around in front of their men.

The anniversary of the Battle of Sedan was also celebrated with the Kaiser-Strasse beflagged from end to end. Always a day of blue sky and sunny lovely weather.

At the time of the wedding of the Hereditary Grand Duke with Princess Hilda of Nassau, Mama was staying at the Hotel Germania in Karlsruhe. Many of the wedding guests were put up at the Hotel as the Castle was already overflowing. There Mama met Doctor Evans, the American Dentist who came to the aid of the Empress Eugenie when she was escaping from Paris. He drove her to the coast on her way to England and safety.

Dr Evans' secretary was a young Frenchman and he escorted Mama around the town on the night of the illuminations, while the Doctor was attending a party at the Castle.

One morning Mama happened to meet Dr Evans outside the Town Hall and he said to her "had you only been passing a minute or two earlier, I would have presented you to the Crown Prince, who is a most homely, kindly man. He was talking with me just now". (The Crown Prince of Germany was married to Queen Victoria's eldest daughter, our Princess Royal. He became Emperor Frederick for a short time.)

The wedding was indeed the cause of a great gathering together of Notabilities. We saw Bismarck, the old Emperor William I, the Crown Prince Frederick and the Emperor's only daughter, Luise, Grand Duchess of Baden. Imagine what a rushing on to the balconies took place then as they drove by so unexpectedly.

Sometime after the wedding the Hereditary Grand Duke was very seriously ill with inflammatory rheumatism and we heard how Princess Hilda ran to the Grand Duchess one day and said "Oh Mother, Father is cross which is a sure sign he is getting better!"

On the eve of St Nicholas, Edward, Frau Nickles son, used to arrive in our schoolroom disguised as St Nicholas, looking rather like an English Father Christmas. On his back he bore a sack loaded with apples and sweetmeats and, in one hand, he held a birch and loud were the shrieks when he strove to apply it, driving us before him. The apples, sweets and cakes for the good girls and the birch for those who had a poor record!!

Our Christmas Eves - how beautiful they were. *Stille Nacht, Heilige Nacht*, solemn and sweet was the singing round the tree and how sweet too, the resin perfume from the boughs when, in the hush and lovely stillness, we were admitted into the Salon.

When New Year came we would rush out on New Year's Eve from the warm rooms, onto the balconies in the clear frosty air, calling out to passers *"Prosit Neu Jahr"* (Happy New Year) and they would call back again to us, echoing the wish. This was always allowed to us on New Year's Eve - the staying up till the New Year arrived.

Every year a Great Fair was held in some of the wide streets, under the shade of the trees and I haven't forgotten the glee I felt when we were allowed to visit the stalls with their thrilling wares. We especially enjoyed seeing waffles made before our eyes on the Waffeln Stall and these, as a great treat, we were able to sample. What fun it was, great crowds of happy people and, in the background, music from the roundabouts. We looked forward to the Fair for weeks and saved up for it.

Oh what a delightful life it was to us carefree girls and no more shivering in winter time because we had porcelain or Majolica stoves which dispensed, without any fuss, a lovely penetrating warmth to every corner of our school till I found, with joy, that I could cheerfully dispense with my English red flannel underwear that I so hated for its ugliness and scratchiness. The marvel is that I wasn't a penny the worse for leaving it off!

It amused us to see the rose trees put into their winter garments in late autumn. Straw contraptions that made them look like "Jacks in the Green", but they needed this protection, the winters of blue sky and sunshine were very cold and oh, with what a wealth of velvety colour and perfume they greeted us each summer.

When Herr Von Heusch and his brother officers dined at the Castle he would bring Mabel and myself little favours from the table. This was quite the usual thing in Germany to take away little mementoes and bon bon for young friends or children.

One summer evening we attended the Dragoons Patrol at the Castle, by special invitation, and I remember the smart officers on parade in their electric blue coats and shining helmets and the scent from the pink Oleanders growing in great tubs by the Castle railings.

One day we were invited by Frau Von Heusch, who was on a visit to her son, to attend a luncheon with some friends of hers. We met an Australian girl called Blance, she was some years older than Mabel and me. She was tall with a dark complexion and fine eyes shaped like swallows wings with heavy dark brows. She had a classical profile with the tiniest tilt of a lovely slender nose and a charming moulded chin. In fact, she was bewitching.

After a crab and white wine lunch Blance played and sang to us and I could see Herr Von Heusch was enchanted by her singing "The Wearing of the Green". I found myself forsaken! "Don't let him see, he's not worth it" whispered Mabel, as with sundry nudges and good natured counsel she tried to draw me from the window, where I stood looking out with what must have been a very tragic expression. My day was ruined and done and all hope lost!

Later, as we were walking in the park, I beside Frau Von Heusche, she suddenly said "Nelly never become a young Welt Dame!" (Young woman of the world.)

Some days later, what did my anxious heart ask itself when I suddenly came face to face with my beloved under the chestnut trees of the Anlage, walking with a comrade? He saluted me with a tragic expression on his pale face. "What have I done?" thought I and searched back with anxiety but could find no cause.

To this day I remember his good looks and the way the bronzed skin in summer used to sharply give way to the beautiful fair white skin where his uniform cap used to rest. I keep seeing his smiling, loving eyes and hear his deep voice again. Oh, how I loved him and I believe he felt for me, but made his head rule his heart as Prussian officers were taught in those days. He told me once that I was his ideal and he always showed me a quiet depth of his feelings.

Herr Von Heusch, my dear, kind, honourable friend, I greet you in my dreams and memories across the years.

Early in the morning on the day that the Black Dragoons were bidding farewell to Karlsruhe on being transferred to Mannheim and Schwetzingen, I was very surprised to be awoken by one of the girls who presented me with a piece of music on which was written, with some formality, "My Name". A Bursch (A Batman) had just brought it and hurriedly handed it in saying "This is for Miss N Bell" and departed. I excitedly unwrapped it and found it to be a pretty little song, what was very popular and tuneful, with fanciful words about fairies weaving their dances in the woodlands while a watcher looked on from their midst, entertained most affectionately by the most beautiful fairy). The sender made a kindly comparison to me with these words.
"My love I thought of you and child believe none were as fair as thee!"

Our schooldays in dear Karlsruhe came to an end in the Summer of 1886.

I remember that last Sunday evening very clearly, when all the leaving girls were gathered together and we sang, with tears rolling down our cheeks, "A few more years shall roll", an English Hymn chosen especially for us by Frau Nickles for our departing.

Before returning to England Mabel and I had hoped to visit Frieburg for a few weeks, drawn there mainly by all we'd heard of its history and interesting surroundings, but, alas, it was not to be as Mama decided we should go to Heidelberg. I've always felt, with regret, that by not going there something was missed from my life!

However, Heidelberg was delightful and we enjoyed our stay with some friends of Papa in their charming house. The view from the front of it was most beautiful, overlooking the old town and river. In the distance were the high Odenwald Hills. The back of the house rose sheer from the Schloss Weg.

Our host was a German Bank Manager with an English wife and three daughters, Loli, Alice and Paula. They were a kind family who made us most welcome. My days with them filled me with enthusiasm and delight and I soon grew to love their quaint old town.

I often wandered up to the summit of the Heilgenberg (Mountain of the Saints) where I would find white heather, and then down the other side I'd go until I came to the Engelwiese (The Angels' Meadow - Longfellow described this meadow in his prose Endymion) which, in summer, was filled with the loveliest wild flowers. I gathered them as I walked and always arrived home with an armful! My route took me across the Necker, on the old bridge, and then I threaded my way through the winding little streets of the ancient town till I climbed up the Schloss - Weg (Castle Way) to my dwelling place.

During our stay we met Frau Ida Von Warble, whose sister was a Lady in Waiting to the Grand Duchess at Court in Baden. She told us that whenever an English parcel arrived the Grand Duchess insisted she was told so that she could open and smell the English smell of its contents!

One summer's evening we were invited by the Principals of Heidleberg College to witness the Illuminations of the Castle from their grounds on the other side of the Necker. That occasion was a magical experience for me - lovely music which filled my heart with joy, fireflies dancing in the dark shadows under the trees and nightingales singing in the woods which adjoined the College gardens.

We often visited the village of Schwetzingen and walked in its lovely park with its groves of purple and white lilac; a tranquil river flowed between green lawns mirroring tall trees.

This park was created in the 18th Century by one of the Markgrafs of Baden for his favourite ladies. A mosque stood in the centre with Arabic lettering on its outer walls proclaiming "Speech is silver and silence gold". There was a dreamy stillness about the whole place. We seldom met others wandering there - time seemed to stand still in that lovely place.

We usually had refreshments at the Golden Lion Inn before catching our train back to Heidelberg. Mine host and his two sisters always made us most welcome to their charming home, which reminded me of a music box house with its flower filled window boxes and colourful shutters.

So ends my memories of those faraway days when I was taken away from a boarding school in Deal and transported to a land of forests, hills, rivers, castles, blue skies, wonderful flowers (especially the roses and lily of the valley), peaches, apricots, wild raspberries and strawberries, goose girls, music and dancing.

When I look back to those happy days I wonder at the marvellous romance of it all and count myself much blessed to have been sent to school in Karlsruhe. I realise that none of these memories will really be lost, they are stored up in my mind and, hopefully, I will be able to travel back through those scenes again, which I found so dear and lovely when I was young.

Schlossberg, 1889

CHAPTER FIVE
RETURN TO GERMANY AND NEW LOVE

Nelly returned to London where she studied at The Royal Academy of Art but part of her remained in Germany. Her first love, the Dragoon Officer, Herr Von Heusch was prevented by his Prussian protocol from a public display of his true feelings for Nelly.

Later, Nelly would learn that Von Heusch never married and that he cherished all her letters. Upon his death in 1933 the letters were returned to her tied together with a silk cord - a lifelong signal of his hidden feelings.

Perhaps it was a thought that she might meet Von Heusch again or simply her affection for the country that drew her back to Germany once more, in 1890. On this occasion she took a holiday in Heidelberg and once again she would meet a man who would change her life.

★ ★ ★ ★ ★ ★ ★ ★ ★ ★

One evening while attending a soirée at the university, I met Harry Fraser Sandeman. He was a good looking young man of twenty. His twinkling blue eyes met mine across the room and soon we were deep in conversation. I found he had a delightful sense of humour and I found myself fascinated.

We had many mutual friends in Heidelberg, so we met on many occasions.

I soon learnt he was a roamer with a sense of adventure which appealed to my young, romantic ideas. His father wanted him to join the family wine business - but Harry had other plans!

When he completed his university course he decided to go to Canada. By this time we'd become good friends and I was rather upset at the thought of him going away - also I was trying to direct my heart away from my German love.

When Harry reached Canada, he journeyed to Alberta, where he at first worked on a ranch in the Calgary area owned by some people called Waldon. He became friendly with their cook, who eventually inherited the title of the Marquis of Queensberry. Harry enjoyed the freedom of the outdoor life and decided he would rent a farm of his own and settle down.

I received a proposal of marriage from Harry early in 1896. It came at the right time for me as I was feeling very unsettled and wondering where my life was leading me.

Much to my parent's horror, I accepted Harry's offer of marriage, (I made my head rule my heart, which I later learnt was a great mistake) and arrangements were made for my journey to Canada.

★ ★ ★ ★ ★ ★ ★ ★ ★ ★

Harry Fraser Sandeman was born in Bombay, India, on 30 November 1870. His father, Roderick Fraser

Sandeman, was educated at Eton and the Royal Military College, Sandhurst. He passed from Sandhurst with a commission and in 1861, at the age of 19 went to Burma and India where he joined a Gurkha Regiment and later the Bengal Lancers.

Whilst in India Roderick met and married Mary Elizabeth Wran a girl ten years his junior - she was seventeen at the time of their marriage.

Mary Elizabeth and Roderick Fraser Sandeman returned to England before the birth of their second child, Ernest Roderick, in 1874. They bought a large house in Maddock Lane, Ealing, West London, a district popular with those returning from service in India.

On his return to civilian life, Roderick Fraser Sandeman entered the business of importing wines from France and Germany. This venture was encouraged by his cousins in the Sherry trade who felt that his military connections would be valuable. The firm was called Page & Sandeman.

The couple went on to have three further children, all daughters; Ruby Mary born in 1880, Maud Wilhelmina born in 1882 and Constance born in 1891. Sadly, in 1898, Mary Elizabeth died at the age of 46. She had been unwell for many years and had spent a long time in a nursing home.

Harry Fraser Sandeman was educated at a small public school and was then sent to a school in Boulogne to become proficient in the French language. In France he became sick to a degree that his health was so impaired that when he applied for admission to Sandhurst he was turned down on medical grounds. In lieu of the Royal Military College he completed his education by attending the university at Heidelberg.

Harry Fraser Sandeman.
"I found myself fascinated."

PART THREE

CANADA.

CHAPTER SIX
WESTWARD HO!

August 18th, 1896 saw me leave the shores of England and sail for Canada where I was to marry Harry Sandeman. I spent many hours of the voyage on deck, sketching and reading.

My first sight of land was when we steamed up the St. Lawrence river. We stopped at Quebec, where I said 'goodbye' to some of my fellow travellers - the Bishop of Edinburgh, Mr. Caffin, Mr. Maynardier and Miss Gates.

The next day we arrived at Montreal at dusk. Lights gleamed out along the river banks. I stood by the rail and watched us dock. Upon landing we had to face the Customs and I passed successfully through after about an hour.

Miss Cane, one of my fellow passengers on the ship, introduced me to her Papa and I was invited to travel in their cab to the Hotel Windsor, where I was to spend the night.

I slept well. After breakfast I went shopping before driving to the Railway Station to board the train which was to carry me three quarters across Canada, to Strathcona, Alberta.

I found that I was to share a parlour car with Mrs. Barrow and her young daughter Lucy, Mrs. Wooley, Mr. and Mrs Pooley and Mr. Griffith. They, like me, were all starting new lives in Canada and we dined together each evening like a family.

I had hardly any sleep on the first night. The train's whistle sounded like a fog horn with a bad cold - or a cow in anguish! I thought of wild monsters when I heard its hoarse screech in the middle of the dark night.

Next morning we passed great forests diversified by lakes in picturesque rocky basins, all very wild and at time depressing in its sameness of rock and undergrowth, with the trees (pines) standing grim and tall against the sky. Heron Bay took my fancy and I longed to stop and explore it. I sat on the platform of the last carriage all morning, at the invitation of Sir Donald Smith. It was a strange feeling to sit there while the train rushed wildly on.

On the 24th of September we passed Lake Superior. It was a wonderful deep blue colour and looked more like the sea than a lake. I had much pleasure watching the waves dashing against the rocks and I felt that I wanted to stop the train and paddle in the clear, cool water.

That evening we dined on Lake Superior trout which was delicious. The sun sank like a fiery ball behind the hills as we ate.

Lovely as it was, the scenery did not please or content me as that of England. I thought that there was too much of it! One was surfeited by it. England is far more restful and I longed for the soft tender colours of its woods in autumn rather than those vivid colours - glorious though they were. There was no restfulness about them, especially where those sentinel pines kept grim watch. Should I ever love or understand them I wondered?

The night before we reached Winnipeg I sleep soundly; in fact I out-slept everyone and was late for breakfast! The beds on the train were most comfortable, with clean snow-white linen every night, and my porter was most kind.

It was raining when we arrived and my spirits were low as I ventured forth with Mrs. Barrow and Lucy for a walk to stretch our legs. I was pleased when it was time to leave that dreary town.

The next few days saw us travelling through a featureless landscape. The prairies were very flat, a land-ocean of black, dry earth as far as the eye could see, with hardly a tree or house in sight. The only redeeming thing about that part of my journey was the wide, wide sky and huge white billowing clouds scurrying across them.

Occasionally we passed a station which reminded me I was in an occupied country. Would I ever get used to such monotonous scenery, I asked myself?

It was already dark when I at last reached Strathcona - a cold, frosty night with a clear, star-filled sky.

Harry met me and drove me to the Strathcona Hotel. We dined together and although I was very tired I managed to enjoy the meal.

The hotel had been built by the Calgary & Edmonton Railway and was opened on 5 December 1891. Strathcona is situated in South Edmonton and dates back to when the Calgary & Edmonton railway tracks were completed on the South side of the North Saskatchewan River. It was named after Lord Strathcona.

I spent the days before my marriage meeting Harry's friends and sightseeing. I did not se my new home until after our wedding - so I had no idea what was in store for me!

Harry and I were married on 21 October at Holy Trinity Church by the Rev. Allan Gray. The church was a small wooden one built by volunteers and completed in October 1893.

We were given a small reception by some friends. The first few days of our married life we spent at the Strathcona Hotel before setting out for the farm.

After our wedding we went to live in an old farmstead called Netherleigh Farm at Leduc. It was built over an old Indian graveyard and was said to be haunted.

At Netherleigh I found a forgotten, neglected garden with broken paling protecting a few marigolds and lemon thyme; mute witnesses of what had happened there. They were a welcome sight to me!

To reach Leduc from Strathcona we travelled by buggy along the Calgary Trail which was a track cut through the trees, with all the stumps left standing and the horses had to avoid them. The only way was to have one wheel see-sawing on top of a stump and the other wheel following from another stump with a shattering bump. So we progressed at a walking pace. (Mr. Gray, a neighbour, used to say what an excellent drive it was for one's liver!) We passed over a little creek which I nicknamed "The

Thames" and the flat packbridge across it, "London Bridge" and so the track continued South West until our farm was reached.

Just beyond us was Telford's Store which sold everything from candles to ribbons! Mr. Telford was our Postmaster and Leduc's first member of Parliament.

Blade was the name of our nearest neighbour on our side of the track and a bit further on, on the opposite side, lived the Mortimers, whom we called 'The Duke and Duchess' because of their regal manners. Mrs. Mortimer was never seen without her hat and a sunshade in summer.

On summer Sundays we would take picnics to various lakes around Leduc. They were kingdoms of loveliness to me after the dry prairie. I loved to gather huge bunches of Silver Buttons and Pretty Ladies which grew profusely at the water edge. Oh those moonlit evenings as we drove home!

The kitchen at Netherleigh Farm, Leduc

★ ★ ★ ★ ★ ★ ★ ★ ★ ★

September 11th, 1897 was the day our first little daughter was born. It was a day of gold and blue and I remember thinking how wonderful it looked, as I lay on a sofa, looking out of the open door to golden leaves, deep blue sky and the little canaries flitting about in the trees.

Little did I know that, before midnight, I would have lost my precious.

LULLABY

Sleep, my baby, sleep and rest thee
More than Mother's care is round thee,
God's own angels bend over thee.
Little ones, like thee, He loves
Little Baby, God doth love thee.
He is love.

He it is, who send the angels
When the stars are twinkling brightly
Come the angels to delight thee
Show thee wonders without ending.
In the lovely land of dreaming
Where the babies gather nightly
Each with its guardian spirit
Gathering flowers until daybreak
In the peaceful land of dreams.
Some there are such weary babies
Yet their mothers come not to them,
Such are these, the loving angels
Take within their arms and cradle
While the angels whisper softly,

"Soon shall baby come to Heaven
Come and live with us in Heaven,
Where no child is sad and lonely
And where every-one finds love."

Leduc, September 1897

* * * * * * * * * * *

The long cold winters of Alberta were a struggle and I was assailed by sickening homesickness. I felt I would never see Dear Green England again.

Once Winter was over I would turn my eyes to Spring and the garden and I felt better. I found the constant whiteness of snow very depressing. Everything buried for months on end and then suddenly one day the snow would start to melt and there was hope and a promise of things to come.

* * * * * * * * * * *

One day in 1898 we were on the banks of the Saskatchewan River, looking Westward and watching a great flood. High above, we stood and watched the surging, relentless water.

Just as we turned away homewards, we heard a shout and, running back, were just in time to see the old "North West" coming swiftly round the bend, proud as a swan borne on by relentless power, a beautiful, stately creature. She seemed human and a Queen.

A queer, pitying cry - half groan, half appeal, rose from the little group assembled on the bank. But nothing could stay her. We heard a fearful, tearing, ripping sound as she struck the breakwaters of the new bridge and rushed on out of our sight. Around a further bend she met her doom.

CHAPTER SEVEN
NEW CENTURY. NEW LIFE.

In 1900, just before the birth of my daughter Eleanor Winifred (Winnie) on 16 July, we moved to Strathcona. Our new home was called Clovernook, such a pretty-looking place that it gave me a very restful feeling when I first saw it. There was nothing grand or pretentious about it - it was just a dear little house built in bungalow style with pretty windows and a verandah and green lawns and flowering beds around it. Trees shaded the house without darkening it and the sunshine fell softly through the leaves.

Clovernook was situated within five minutes' walk of the carlines yet so near the bush that a few steps took one into the wilderness where Nature had her way. In Summer shrubs burst with a wealth of blossom and wild flowers gemmed the grass. Birds nested, fluttering and calling to each other, all day long. When the evening shadows lengthened the nightly song programme of the musical frogs blended with other sounds of nature.

Within our garden, robins nested in the tall Balm of Gilead trees and nowhere in the world could they have been more secure - as the mistress of the house was (and still is) an ardent lover of birds and animals.

In June the climbing roses grew visibly, from dawn to dusk and again from dark to dawn. Ah no! It is not correct to use the term 'dark', for in Strathcona there is no dark in mid Summer. The lingering luminance of the sunset travels over the sky to meet the awakening dawn. There is no night.

The blue forget-me-nots in my flower beds lifted their innocent heads in wonderful profusion and the lilac in full bloom invited one to bury one's face in their clusters to inhale the delicious fragrance within.

I was never happier than when I was amongst my beloved flowers; bending over than or kneeling to weed them was a great joy. One friend said I reminded her of Elizabeth in her German Garden - but with a difference as she never worked in her garden, she just looked at it!

Harry's eldest sister, Ruby, came from England to stay just before Eleanor was born. She helped us move house and assisted me with my new daughter. She arrived in May 1900 having travelled on the SS Tunisian, an Allan Line ship which sailed from Southampton on April 5th to Halifax and then on by train.

Soon after her arrival she met John McFarland, a struggling grain merchant. It is difficult to understand what they found in common. His family was poor and his education limited but he had, while working, put himself through Business School and was an avid reader. Ruby with her good looks and background bowled him over and Harry and I sensed what was about to happen.

John had come to Strathcona from Winnipeg to form a new company, The Alberta Grain Co. He was backed in this venture by N.J. Bawff and also by Premier Roblin of Manitoba. Connie told us she felt in her bones John would do well and this was so.

They were married from our house on 15 October 1901 and in the course of time three sons were born, the first, Ernest Roderick in 1903.

Our son, Roderick Fraser was born on 20 May 1903. Eleanor was very pleased to have a living doll to play with and enjoyed helping me to look after him!

Boating in Banff

We started going to Banff for Summer holidays. When the children were young they enjoyed the train journey and eagerly looked forward to seeing the mountains again.

What happy days they were; picnics, canoeing, walking and a log cabin house, which we rented near the river, to live in. We rose early and went to bed late, all our meals were eaten out of doors and we grew brown and healthy in the bracing mountain air - so different to the searing, tiring heat of Strathcona.

Eleanor and Roderick in the garden at Strathcona

★ ★ ★ ★ ★ ★ ★ ★ ★

Harry established a Real Estate business in 1899 on Whyte Avenue, Strathcona and farming was forgotten. In 1909, E.H. Cope joined him and it became the Sandeman-Cope Co. Ltd. and two new branches were opened in London and Glasgow.

Harry became a Councillor on the Strathcona Council and also played cricket for the town's team.

Sandeman-Cope's Real Estate Office, 1910

* * * * * * * * * *

When I look back, what remains is the little wren's song and the scent of the red wild roses in June as we followed the winding way of the Calgary Trail (from Leduc to South Edmonton) and the yellow-gold of leaves against the deep blue sky of September and the little, wild, yellow canaries flitting amongst the trees. The white blossom in Spring of Saskatoon and wild cherry against the intense blue of the sky over the lake and the cold of Winter with the glitter of great diamonds among the branches powdered with hoar frost.

What remains longest is the wren's sweet, homely song.

PART FOUR

ENGLAND ONCE MORE.

CHAPTER EIGHT
NOTES FROM APPLEDORE, 1928.

After the birth of her children Nelly's life went into something of a decline. Not that she wasn't a loving and caring mother. She took great pleasure in her children and in their development. However, as much as she enjoyed her garden at Clovernook she was always homesick in Canada.

Events were to ensure that Nelly would return to England. Harry Sandeman's Real Estate business failed and in 1917 the family moved to Ealing in West London.

As her children grew up so her marriage crumbled and by 1924 Nelly started a series of journeys to those parts of England she remembered from her childhood. She wandered through her beloved Sussex and Kent staying in a variety of delightful cottages, tending gardens, walking in woods and meadows, visiting churches and all the time observing and writing down what she saw.

These notes from Appledore were set down in 1928, Nelly's daughter Winnie is far away in Canada and her friend and neighbour, the actress Ellen Terry dies. Despite the solitude Nelly continues to take immense joy from nature.

"To lift my eyes from the soil of living and behold the patient stars: to feel a little wind come cooling and fresh caressing my face, is bliss to me".

* * * * * * * * * *

Appledore weather, which to me means summer weather, warm with a blissfully blue sky and a strong breeze blowing. A sweet-sour apple with a tang to it - Appledore weather. They don't know what I mean when they say - "a beautiful day?" and I answer. "Yes. *Appledore weather*!"

How should they know that these Summer days seem to have fallen to me from lost days, dropped out of my childhood's Summer days of holiday that should have been fine but took on inky tints of gloom in sea and sky; while the *real* years hid themselves away, stored themselves up for the last years to be. So that sitting by the wayside amidst the waving grasses with scent of white clover and elder-blossom coming in happy waves and wafts of warm perfume - I must needs think, it was just like this, when I was a child; surely the long years behind are a dream. They are not far-off who made life secure and I rest under their protection still.

Just so the sun used to shine; just so was the sky so blissfully blue and the breeze so sweet and so keen. Appledore weather!

* * * * * * * * * *

And again that strange sense as of return to past days. Last evening, walking through the hayfields and pausing to let tired eyes dwell with wistful love, on that distant soft line of blue that led to the Kentish cliffs - lit up here and there with a twinkling star of intense light, reflection of the setting sun on little, homely windows - again it came, the sense of love, warm, true and old-fashioned (yes, old-fashioned) and so almost without knowing it, I found myself singing the refrain of a little song, which rose unbidden through the mists of memory. There was no-one to hear on the wide marshlands, so over and over again, the tender, lilting refrain repeated itself. The simple words brought with them a sense of comfort and of restoration, spoke again of love and eternal things.

Tired out with study and quest, the mind roaming out into the homeless space, I came back to the child's unquestioning faith and knowledge, back, I think, to the Everlasting Arms, which in that golden evening light surely enfolded us all.

★ ★ ★ ★ ★ ★ ★ ★ ★ ★

The bees and the butterflies are busy with the lavender in the tiny garden patch, so I know it must be ready to gather and send away across the Atlantic Ocean to a loved one, carrying the sweetness of an English Summer over those weary leagues of land and sea which divide us.

★ ★ ★ ★ ★ ★ ★ ★ ★ ★

Our neighbour, Ellen Terry, has left us.

Lovely vision of the past, she lives in my mind as Margaret. Margaret, tripping down the stage of the old Lyceum. Out of church she came, across the great square. What? A grandmother? She that vision of youthful grace, that inimitable loveliness, that voice of charm! And so I shall always remember her.

★ ★ ★ ★ ★ ★ ★ ★ ★ ★

The little pale amethyst thistles are blooming again. I had to bend down and smell them; they smell so entrancingly sweet. They remind me of sweet sultan - one of the perfumes of Paradise.

★ ★ ★ ★ ★ ★ ★ ★ ★ ★

Nelly loved to revisit the Kent of her childhood. Here she paints "the last of the old houses of Deal beach."

It is late, all the good Appledore folk are in bed. All that is but I. The last light went out hours ago - but I love to stay up in the quiet and peace and think of them all asleep; and the house-martins tucked up in their nests, so close to their human friends.

My room with its low ceiling, worm-eaten beams and tiny casement window is so stiflingly hot tonight that I dread going upstairs. Instead, I wish that this cottage could tell its story, while all is quiet and Appledore steeped in rest profound. When the worn, uneven brick floor was, a few years ago, they found beneath, a silver penny of Henry VII's day.

Faircross Cottage, a strangely beautiful name! It is said that the ancient Village Cross once stood outside, and on the little Green the Fair was held by the Fair Cross.

Had I but the power of absorbing from the atmosphere, some story quaint and olden; but alas, decay and neglect have wrought their evil work. A sweet but untended rose, with great, heavy, pink blooms, climbs up beside the old green door and speaks to me of perished care - mutely asking leave to go on bearing roses, and for support for its fragrant buds. But I must away to bed for there's either a Banshee or cat wailing outside amongst the lavender bushes - and its ghostly company!

★ ★ ★ ★ ★ ★ ★ ★ ★ ★

A little old lady lives next door to me, in Old Way cottage: a frail, little, snowy-haired, blue-eyed gentlewoman. She tends her roses and weeds her garden despite her many years.

She has a well-bred, white, Highland Terrier and I own a little brown Terrier (whom I dearly love) and when these two little dogs happen to be looking out of their respective casement windows upstairs, surrounded by rose sprays and plum tree branches you might be forgiven for rubbing your eyes, as you passed by our lavender-sweet front gardens - rubbing your eyes and asking yourself, have you strayed into the land of Nursery Rhyme and what beneficent Old Mother Hubbards dwell in Old Way Cottage and Faircross Cottage, with a dog apiece?

★ ★ ★ ★ ★ ★ ★ ★ ★ ★

A gold embroidery of tall, swaying buttercups borders the Old Way - a forgotten, grassy lane now (given over to the Villager's potsherds and petrol cans and other tokens of poor husbandry) - it was once an important highway - the ancient way across Romney Marsh.

Romney Marsh has a great fascination for me - my feet wend there instinctively. To wander in the quiet, winding, willow lanes, lifts my spirits and rest me mentally - it is always so peaceful there.

To my fancy, Appledore seems somewhat like a moated village, as you look across the water from the flat pasture lands. Little, tree-shadowed river - you are in reality, a canal, the Military Canal - but how hard and harsh for your Swan-haunted stream. How serenely flows the water at the foot of Appledore, save where the wind at the bend of the river flicks it into ripples of crisp and shining light. Gently the land rises beyond, and where once sea-water lapped against the shore, it is now velvety green and tree shadowed.

On the higher ground and sheltered by great trees, the church appears, seeming to disclose itself half reluctantly to the stranger, who comes upon it unexpectedly and finds, to his delight, a picture for his contemplation, church, trees and a stretch of river, holding in its smooth waters, as in a clear mirror, the reflection of summer skies; the dark, heavy foliage of the wych-elms, with their drooping branches; the velvet-seeming green of high banks whereon the sheep are feeding and the long, low, ancient church embowered with trees.

★ ★ ★ ★ ★ ★ ★ ★ ★ ★

How could I think, when I first wandered here, that Appledore had little to tell of the past? How much there is to gather up, like those "fragments that remained", if we just paid attention.

The Danes wintered here in the estuary in 893 AD, striking heaven alone knows what terror into the hearts of the people, fleeing for shelter beneath the snow-laden boughs of the Andredswold - with what poor homely treasure they could snatch up as they fled.

The Black Death was a grim visitor to Appledore. Among the names of Rector and Vicars of the village you will find inscribed in the church:

1348-9	Luke Gerard }	The Black Death
1349	Adam de Sythington }	

So they handed in their resignations to that grim spectre and with them went how many more of Appledore, through that Dark Valley? After these two it seems as if no-one came to minister to the people who were left, until 1366. Had the flock so dwindled, that there was no need of a shepherd?

One, Philip Chute, Standard-Bearer to Henry VIII, was buried in this old Church of St. Peter and St. Paul. Much

I wondered in which house he may have dwelt, until I found that Horne Place was his home, a home gained by the loss of another in Elizabeth I's reign. Horne Place passed through an heiress to a Guldeford who, refusing the Oath of Supremacy, had to flee abroad, when the estate was forfeited to the Crown and conferred on Philip Chute, Captain and Standard-Bearer at Boulogne.

Where in the church his body rests, no-one knows. Is it in the Horne Chapel, under that worn, roughened old stone beneath the Communion Table? April is often cruel, bringing sleet-laden, cutting winds, but the 7th of April , 1566 brought, (it is just a fancy) a spring morning of tender, budding green, with the blackbirds fluting, when the old Standard-Bearer of the King was carried to his last resting place.

Did Godfrey the Butcher crave to be buried in the South Aisle, (as he was in 1518), because the sun shines in so warmly there? We walk by his tomb today and looking down, see the sturdy figure of Robert Godfrey, outlined with his implements of butchery. We scarce miss the vanished brasses, which once filled the empty spaces.

What manner of man was Mr. Hemmings - Chaplain to Colonel Pride, 1655? Here is room for conjecture. Was he a sour-faced fanatic who wrought almost as much destruction in the church as the French did, in 1380, or had he a secret leaven of his own, that inclined him to sympathy with the dispossessed? Did he close the church on Christmas Day and denounce the bright-berried holly? Or was he a tired man and gentle, endowed of understanding and weary of dispute? We cannot ever know, but somehow I picture him kindly.

Like a tired child, seeking its Mother, that it may sit at her feet and, leaning against her knee, feel sure of security and love - so go I, to the little church of Appledore in the early morning. Too tired and with nothing to hope or pray for - I go, as to my Mother's knees and kneel there in peace and security - not looking or asking for any favour or kindness but to rest in *good company.*

"Our Lady of Pity" - whom did she pity I mused? Shipwrecked folk afar from home, and those souls whose earthly encasements, torn from them by the sea and tossed by the wrath of the waves upon these shores, were brought to her, perchance, and laid at her feet. And those who, stealing humbly in though the half-opened door, confessed to her their very human sins.

As I sat there alone, in the dim light of late evening, into my quiet, unoccupied mind, stole gently as the murmuring of the wind, as the rustling of the leaves - like a stream of wistful music floating one knew not whence, these haunting words: *"Some of them have dwelt a long time in Paradise"*.

★ ★ ★ ★ ★ ★ ★ ★ ★ ★

The Lady of Pity looketh down for ever upon the sound of Prayer.

"Grant Me, I pray
One dewdrop from thy willow spray
And in the double lotus keep
My hidden heart asleep."

★ ★ ★ ★ ★ ★ ★ ★ ★ ★

July

My walks at the moment are perfumed with clover, meadow sweet, elder-blossom, wild roses and honey-suckle. Today I walked far and had long views of Marsh and Sky and the distant, blue hills towards Folkestone. How lucky I am to have all the Romney Marsh to explore and look upon.

At one time I walked along a winding lane, easy to the feet but very lonely. Here and there I passed a farmstead and orchards. In one orchard were old-fashioned beehives, all such a pleasure to my eyes. I made bold efforts to reach the sea but a big, black Angus cow foiled me, at what you might say was my last lap! It galloped up - so I retired to the nearest gate and shut it in its face. I was very relieved when I saw the sign of matronhood!

On my way home I crossed many fields enclosed with great ivy-clad Elms. Everywhere looked so peaceful - such a lovely bit of Old England and so loved by me.

★ ★ ★ ★ ★ ★ ★ ★ ★ ★

All day it had rained on and off, dreary and grey. Going out in the heavy showers to walk - heart-sick at ill news and eyes downcast - I had reached the quiet willow lane (dear, lonely sanctuary away on the Marshes) bordered with old willows of singular size and beauty. There, looking up once more at the grey, unpromising heavens, suddenly I saw before me, a great rainbow span - unfailing promise and fulfilment!

★ ★ ★ ★ ★ ★ ★ ★ ★ ★

I like the Marsh Folk - they are kindly people. A farmer gave me a lift to Brookland today in his cart: ("Get up Tom. I bred him myself, Mum!")

Yes they planted the willows by the dykes to show the side of the road or they'd have been driving into the water on dark night.

"They're not Bulrushes - they're *Pokers*. Town folk call them Bulrushes, but they don't know. I'll show you what a true Bulrush is. There aren't many of them about, but if you go down by that row of trees, and through a gate to your left and keep on a little way, you'll find the true Bulrushes in a little hollow.

That bird Mum? Why that's a Lapwing - the marshland is full of Lapwings."

* * * * * * * * * * *

I love the reeds,
The criss-cross charm of them,
Low as they bend to the long dyke's brim,
Swaying and bowing
Their long tresses sweeping,
Grace and enchantment
At the West Wind's whim.

* * * * * * * * * * *

On the Fairfield Road, on a bit of forgotten hedge, by chance protected, I found the little creamy flowers of the Burnet Rose; that pretty little wild rose with its clusters of buds on madder-brown stems.

Close by, sailed out from their nesting place in the reeds of the great dyke, a Swan family - a proud father and mother and seven little, grey cygnets.

When I walked this way in early June, I came across a bill nailed on an old field gate, advertising lands for sale in neighbouring parishes. Lands in *"Fairfield, Becketsland, Cherrytown, Kenardington, Brookland and Appledore."* Where else, but in our little England, are villages with such singing names? Today I went that way again, armed with pencil and notebook to copy out exactly that jingle of fair names - but alas, a rough wind had blown the "song" away.

★ ★ ★ ★ ★ ★ ★ ★ ★ ★

I was told today of a *character,* a tramp called "Canal Jack", who used to spend his time tramping up and down the canal banks from Hythe to Appledore. "But he's gone beyond it now," said the little woman.

I do not wonder at his tramping there; the old man must have loved it, taking his way through the avenue of trees, on one side of him the canal, and on the other a little stream or dyke, masses of beautiful glowing colour - pink, crimson, purple and mauve flowers grow undisturbed by the water's edge and here and there, like a bit of the blue Summer's sky fallen and tangled, amidst the lush growth of the waterside, you find a very pool of forget-me-nots.

Great elms spread fan-wise along the course of the canal - a double row of them forming a shady avenue on the high, green banks. Here and there, an ash grows amongst them and, bordering an old, forgotten road below, you find ancient hollies all cherry with their scarlet berries and glossy leaves.

★ ★ ★ ★ ★ ★ ★ ★ ★ ★

August

Doris and I walked to the river on Sunday evening and sat on the bank watching the Swallows (who will be leaving us soon), and one lonely Swan, looked wretched and dejected as it came around the river-bend - crying, crying, - opening its beak and looking from side to side as if it had lost its mate. (You know that Swans are faithful.) It made us very sad. We could see there was something wrong: on it floated downstream, still looking from side to side, seeking vainly, and our eyes followed it with pity, till at length we saw the last of it far away, turning the southward bend - I have never seen a Swan look so miserable. They are all wild swans here. A week or two ago, I noticed three Swans on another stretch of the river. One poor thing, when it ventured to draw near the other two was driven back by one of the pair who went hissing at it with its great wings curved and arched. Maybe it was the same bird as we saw on Sunday.

Appledore-cum-Swanington it should be called! You might be living in a Grimm's Fairy Tale instead of a little English village.

A *vision* of Swans coming and going over the valley. "A sign, a portent," I thought at first when towards dusk one evening I met with seven Swans floating downstream, one behind the other, like a stately fleet. But when another day I met eighteen beautiful, snowy-white Swans gliding through the water in single file close together, beak almost touching tail - I abandoned that idea! Still more so later when I counted twenty-two!

Swans on the river, swans flying away over the marshes and returning not again, the little colony dwindling in size daily. Where go these beautiful birds? Two lovely swans arose from the water yesterday and flew almost over my head. Far away I watched them go.

Today, I saw three take flight together and then came a family of them sailing proudly through the water, seven young swans with father and mother bearing down-stream towards me. Suddenly they took to their wings and flew away seaward.

★ ★ ★ ★ ★ ★ ★ ★ ★ ★

September

The Summer is drawing to its close.

How beautiful is this evening in the mellow light; but there is a wistfulness. All the quick, young life has gone from the pastures.

The work of the Hookers (a Romney Marsh name for Shepherds), disappeared in a day. The young sheep have been taken to warmer, upland pastures in preparation for colder weather, leaving their staid mothers to winter on the Marsh and to repeat their homely pageant next Spring.

★ ★ ★ ★ ★ ★ ★ ★ ★ ★

To lift my eyes from the soil of living and behold the patient stars: to feel a little wind come cooling and fresh caressing my face, is bliss to me.

★ ★ ★ ★ ★ ★ ★ ★ ★ ★

October

October has arrived and there is a dreamy beauty across the river through the thinning, gold-green leaves of wych-elms. The little church appears with an expression so remote, so other-worldly, that my fumbling pencil and brush cannot render it.

The Swans fly over the village in file, their long necks outstretched, their strange cries bidding us to look upward.

The Gypsies' carts stop outside the Forge, the patient ponies wait their masters' pleasure. Michaelmas daisies are blooming in every garden and pale moon-daisies, so delicate and pale, like flower pearls with faint green centres.

* * * * * * * * * *

What a beautiful year it has been to watch. From the time the April lambs came to the Winchelsea Marshes, from blackthorn blossoming; on into May with shiny buttercup gold and scent of hawthorn all-pervading; on into June, with yellow Iris crowding at the river's brink. Wild roses and honeysuckle in the hedges; plumey meadow-sweet by the waterside; the heavy, sweet tang of Elder-blossom in winding marshlands. Haymaking and the little lambs grown older, set apart by themselves like children sent to boarding school - they gleamed whitely in the quiet pastures, resting at eventide - lambs lying down together under the stars in the peace and safety of English meadows.

Now the harvest of the hedges is ripening fast. The sloes, so plentiful this year, with their blue grape-like fruit; the lavish coral of hips and red hawthorn berries and black elder-berries.

★ ★ ★ ★ ★ ★ ★ ★ ★ ★

Cold, cold, blows the wind - the year grows old; her garments are outworn.

★ ★ ★ ★ ★ ★ ★ ★ ★ ★

PART FIVE

A SUSSEX POSY.

CHAPTER NINE
PEASMARSH. CATKINS HANG THEIR TASSELS.

Her daughter Eleanor Winifred had returned to Canada and was married, Roderick was married to Doris and remained in England and so he was able to visit Nelly from time to time. These visits apart, Nelly spent most of her time with only her faithful dog, "Nellie" and her beloved countryside for company.

The solitude suited her well as we learn from "A Sussex Posy", Nelly's diary for 1930, when she lived at Roselands Cottage, Peasmarsh.

* * * * * * * * * * *

"Goe not halfe-way to meet a coming sorowe
Butte thankful bee
For blessing of to-day
And pray that thou mayest blessed be to-morrowe
So shalt thou goe with joy upon thy way."

This must be the motto of the little house, I think. I found it on the tea-pot stand. The more often I read it, the better I like it.

* * * * * * * * * * *

And so we have come back to SUSSEX! Last Summer and Autumn are as if they have never been. I am taking up my life here very nearly where I dropped it last April, when the Dog and I said goodbye to the little house. Far have we gone and much have we learned since then.

★ ★ ★ ★ ★ ★ ★ ★ ★ ★

Jan. 14th.
Today as I passed down the road, my gaze fastened itself upon the deeply flooded valleys and the hills of Kent beyond. Some spell had drawn my eyes far away over bare woodlands and drowned pastures to a headland jutting out boldly into the levels. As I gazed at this point (which for me always holds a strange fascination) I saw a Winter Rainbow born.

Out of the gray sky spaces, the rainbow colours glimmered faintly, wavered, till the perfect arch, springing on one side from the very foot of the headland and growing brighter as I watched it - framed in like a picture, the beloved land. Quietly it came - impressed itself upon the gray, glowed and suddenly faded, like the Kingdom of Heaven which cometh without observation.

Jan. 15th.
Tonight I knelt by my bedroom window, a little diamond-paned casement which overlooks the garden. One star shone over the garden and the moon was coming up. To look out into the garden you *must* kneel, because the kindly thatch comes down so low. On the panes of wavy old greenish glass in one casement a name is scratched - "Ann" in beautiful tall old-fashioned lettering. (Did "Ann" I wonder sometimes kneel to look out of this window on moonlit night centuries ago?) Who owned the orchard then? And did the vanished

cottage down the lane shelter one whom Ann loved, the length or more of her garden away.

> *"Why did she love him, curious heart be still,*
> *Is human love the growth of human will?*
> *To her he might be gentleness."*
>
> Byron

Jan. 16th.
Hazel catkins are hanging their pale green tassels on Tillingham Hill and today I gathered violets in the garden. Out by the little back gate we went, the dog and I, together through fields, over stiles into the great woods, determined to find the firs which always elude me. The trees are winter-stripped and they betrayed the hidden fir-wood in their midst - so I found it at last! How often have I sought it in vain, when all was green. Beautiful and still were its dim aisles, sloping steeply down to a mysterious valley - wrapped in a twilight of their own. Deep down, runs a little, rippling Sussex brook and the late afternoon sunlight finding there a quiet pool, struck from it a jewel-like radiance which glittered between the dusky aisles of the firs. This might be an enchanted forest, a sanctuary for healing, so still, so sweet, so *lost* it is.

I dragged back with me a great fir branch that the late, rough gales must have snapped off. How many years was it growing for this - to bring the staunch green of the firwood into my little house?

Jan. 17th.
A rainy day - pouring with rain, but long rubber boots carried me through pools, brooks and swampy place into the woods.

It is long since I saw the little Sussex water courses so full, rushing and babbling along with such importance, down hill and round corners, headlong over miniature falls - the water a thick, muddy yellow from the clay. "Oh, don't be in such a haste", I cried. "You'll soon be lost in the sea."

For colour, the woods held every note of rain-washed brown, dun, ochre, beechen russet and sombre green. No gold today - but every twig, branch and spray was gemmed with crystal drops. No pale green of bracken today - for last year's fern is a wrecked thing, a drowned thing, most pitiful. Bent and broken stems like white stripped bones, dragged down at sharp angles by the sodden red-brown masses, drenched and mingling with the dead leaves of the forest, in utter degradation.

Can it be possible, that through this soaking mess of what was once pure beauty - new life will pierce, forcing its way unerringly to the surface - eager to cover up the Winter's insult with the miracle of Spring?

As if to answer this question it suddenly ceased to rain so pitilessly, the clouds broke away and as I reached the little house and stood by the garden gate, the answer and a promise was revealed.

To what could one liken it, how labour words to describe the shimmer and the shine of that great Bow in the clouds, surely compounded by the essence of all the flowers that have bloomed on earth, bloomed and passed, even as the living arch, a Rainbow, blooms and passes.

It rose from the ground close, so close to the little cottage, seemingly from beneath the nearby hedge; then arching towards the Valley. I glimpsed the trees of the further woods though its veil of quivering celestial light.

Once as I walked alone by night through the lanes of Iden, between woods in faint moonlight when May was giving place to June - I saw what I took to be a ground mist rising beneath the trees. Looking closer I found it to be a ground mist of Bluebells, luminous masses of moonlit wild Hyacinths making their presence known, like a fairy enchantment to beguile the solitary traveller.

I love those green lanes of Iden, for me they hold a soothing power. There it seems always as if I am not walking alone, unaccompanied in the darkness. But as if a little warm circle of light is about me (invisible to other eyes) or rather, as if the glow of a little lantern accompanies me.

Two marvellous things I have seen since I lived here: the "mist of luminous wild Hyacinths" and the faery Rainbow in the wintery weather.

Jan. 20th

There is a perfect Rose in bloom in the garden. I can see it from my bedroom window under the thatch. Today I brought marigolds in, to light the dark, quiet rooms - for marigolds (like big Summer clovers) never mind being picked but a January Rose feels differently. Since she had the courage to bloom in her creamy perfection, her tawny heart glowing as if it were June, she shall bloom out her life untouched by me.

Jan. 21st.

The ground was white with hoar frost this morning, yet in the sheltered borders snowdrops are showing and a pink primrose blooms. What luck have I to find new treasures every Winter day.

In this old cottage where my dog and I dwell alone, there are two staircases. One I maintain belongs to Sleeping Beauty. Up just such uneven, steep, winding old stairs must Briar Rose have climbed to reach the forgotten chamber where the malevolent fairy sat spinning.

Last Winter was bitterly cold and Sleeping Beauty's staircase sheltered many little dormant butterflies, clinging to the wall all through the hard weather. Frail Psyches asleep, their wings close-folded, like little prayerful hands. But for them no Prince's awakening kiss; a subtler message reached them In their dark abode.

Jan. 27th.
Someone brought me Christmas Rose today -exquisite flowers. I found a humble Butterbur in blossom in a ditch and its almond perfume fills my living room.

Jan. 28th.
Today at Noon I was busy in my oak-beamed kitchen when I heard a knock at the outer door and the dog barked loudly, excitedly. I called out "come in", thinking it my neighbour on some errand. But no one entered at my bidding, yet the knocking continued. Believing at last that it must be a surprise visitor from London - I called out again, "come in, do come in" and then, "who is it - who is it?" (half laughing). A strangely wistful voice answered. "It's only me." I rushed to the door, the dog with me still barking, but there was no one there when I opened it!

My neighbour afterwards assured me that she had not called. The voice was so strangely humble and wistful. *"It's only me."* As if fearful of its welcome. It was a young woman's voice, clear and low with sorrow in it.

Jan. 29th.
The Hunt passed by this morning, green and pink. I was standing at my open front door when the Huntsmen and Hounds went by. A pretty sight but I do not approve of their sport and my heart is with their prey!

How very sweet the old Boxwood hedge is in the early morning. As you brush by, it gives forth its poignant old-world fragrance to the fresh, moist air. There is but a bit of the great hedge left near the wood-lodge door and it must be bewilderingly old, for Box takes so long to grow and this is so high and thickset with such a gnarled and twisted stock.

Feb. 2nd.
I went out to tea at a cottage in Peasmarsh today called "Lavender". It is a very old cottage and has by its front door a large Rosemary bush (you know the old Elizabethan saying, "Plant Rosemary at your door and you'll never lack friends").

On one of the cottage's outer walls there is a most interesting thing I've never seen before.

A love-letter box with 'MW 1731' carved upon it. Centuries ago it was the custom that when a young woman was being seriously courted - a box was made and hung outside for her faithful swain to put his love-letters to her in.

Feb. 10th.
I walked with the dog to Beckley this afternoon to see the Butcher, Mr. Skinner, a very nice young man with a clean, artistically arranged shop.

The road leads through woods nearly all the way - so I kept Nellie on her lead or she might have run away after a rabbit or two into a snare or trap. There are miles of woods around Peasmarsh. I've never seen anything like them in England before.

This corner of Sussex is very lovely, heartachingly so!

Feb. 13th. St. Valentine's Eve.
Little antique frosted glass bowls amber coloured hold bunches of snowdrops (Candlemas Bells, as old Pilbeam the gardener tells me his mother used to call them) in my living room tonight and I've lighted the candles and the little house is warm and cosy and seems as though it's waiting for someone. But no one comes! Yet maybe an unbidden guest may enter unseen. Who can tell how many such steal into a quiet room warm with firelight glow and light of candles and very sweet with innocent flowers.

It might seem like a little sanctuary to them, who have so far to go. And there's pity and love for them and heart's welcome too.

Mar. 1st. St. David's Day.
I have just fed the birds with dripping, bread and cut-up apples. An old one-legged Thrush comes every day and the greedy Starlings. I have had Field Fares lately (a sort of Norwegian Thrush). The local people call them "Grey Birds". They are very timid.

I have a favourite feathered friend "little Teddy Masker", I call him. He's a sort of Tit, dressed in dark blue velvet with a matching cap and a curious grey-white mask and a long tail.

Mar. 5th.
I have a butterfly living with me this Winter, a beautiful little butterfly - such a soft brown furry body and lovely cream and velvety brown wings chequered with blue on the edges and fairy wands of antennae.

I found it first on New Year's Day under a wooden shelf in my sitting room, it was hanging on the support. I was delighted and always took great care when dusting, not to flick its pretty wings or otherwise disturb it.

One day at the end of January I saw it fluttering on the window. The sky was a Summer blue outside and the warmth of the sun had awakened my butterfly.

Then came a freezing night and I thought it would die there in the cold window, but no, it was alive next morning and I put honey out in a little saucer for it. Roddy wanted to put it back in the corner but I wouldn't let him touch it. Next day it walked about on my bare arm and I returned it to the shelf.

Then came day when it was missing and I grieved. I was afraid the dog had caught it or the curious fingers of the child of the woman who scrubs the kitchen floor.
Days passed but no butterfly returned to hang beneath the shelf and I felt a little empty place.

One day as I was hurriedly dressing to go out - I saw something on my bedroom floor, like a little brown leaf, close to the bed. Subconsciously I wondered what it was and touched it and saw, to my delight, a flutter and opening of wings. My Butterfly was safe.

For many days it lingered with me in my bedroom, quite

content when I held it, its wonderful fairy wand antennae examining me.

Alas, one day I found it dying and I lifted it up gently on to the sunlit window ledge. Arranged on the ledge was a bowl of sweet scented narcissi and some of the petals had fallen and I put my Butterfly on to them. It stretched its wings for one last glad flutter and cuddled on the white petals. When I next looked the Psyche (the Greek personification of the soul) had flown far away to the Blue leaving the beautiful wings and the fairy wand antennae folded away in the neatest fashion. It was enough to comfort me to see the composure.

Mar. 12th.
I noticed crowds, no, whole constellations of Celandines on the banks of Bixley Lane as I walked with Nellie today. I was almost startled by the hundreds of bright blue Speedwell "eyes" looking at me as I rounded a corner. Their blue was so intense and unwinking. Each flower glowing. I thought they were like the eyes of little lost children greeting with joy their return to the beautiful earth in the Resurrection of Spring. I have never seen anything so confident of this and it stirred in me a depth beyond words - so joyous was the deep glowing blue out of the sober toned earth.

Mar. 16th.
Today I walked to Wittersham and back. It was a lovely walk, seven miles altogether which I took slowly.

The cleanliness of Wittersham struck me as well as its lovely peace. First I went into the churchyard, to find the grave of Sir Kingsmill Key (a distant cousin of mine). Then though the open door into the church which was full of sunlight. It must be quite old, but in the short visit I was able to pay it there was no trace of its age that I could see and an extraordinary absence of memorial tablets which are usual in an old church.

There is a war memorial tablet on one wall. Today there were yellow narcissi exquisitely arranged and so fresh I felt they had just been placed there. The words of the tablet struck me with their beauty.

> *"Nothing is here for tears, nothing to wail*
> *Or knock the breast, no weakness, no contempt,*
> *Dispraise or blame, nothing but well and fair,*
> *And what may quiet us in a death so noble."*
>
> *Milton*

And in one corner, not far away but in what was once I think a Lady Chapel and is now used for Communion, there is the same lovely touch of blue that I so love in the Horne Chapel at Appledore Church and in that corner pushed right against the walls in the angle was a large bunch of white lilies, a great cluster of lilies. There was an air of reticence about this - as indeed pervades the whole quiet church.

Before starting my walk home, I went to look at old Inn Cottage which is almost opposite the Church. It was once home of the Keys. It is a very long two-storied building, nicely kept up. It was once an Inn.

There are some lovely old houses scattered about in this beautiful backwater. I hope their owners appreciate them. I think they do as they are all so excellently kept up with flower-filled gardens.

Mar. 17th. St. Patrick's Day.
Today is my birthday and the lanes are full of little primroses. They are everywhere. I walked with Nellie to the top of the hill and saw Stone Cliff as it is called jutting out at the point of Oxney Island where now the marshes are instead of sea.

How blessed I am to be living in such a beautiful tract of country.

Mar. 20th.
Through the centuries man and maid must have walked down these dear green lanes as I saw them today, pacing slowly along content in each other's company - so once went William and Margery, John and Prudence, Roger and Clarinda and Peter with Ann. The maids carrying round bunches of Primroses, edged with their soft green crumpled leaves, held so carefully before them, like little bridal bouquets.

So they walked together in sweet converse hundreds of years ago and do still walk as I have seen them in Sussex today and many Springs.

Yes, Celts, Saxons and Normans doubtless in their day they all went a-primrosing with their chosen Maidens.

Mar. 29th.
Today I woke to clear blue skies and warm sun and I made up my mind to try to find the Daffodil Wood - and I did! It is between here and Beckley. You have to approach Beckley for about a mile and then turn down a secluded lane and walk a further one and a half miles till at last where the woodcutters have cut down many trees you see thousands of Wild Daffodils. What a breathtaking sight. Daffodils as far as my marvelling eyes could see.

All in bloom together and dancing in the breeze. Really wild - old English Daffodils - Lent Lilies - sweet, sweet flowers - far daintier than the garden ones and paler in colour. I could not cease to marvel at the wonder of them.

Apr. 3rd.
A green haze has spread itself over the woodlands around Peasmarsh and here and there little saplings are lit up as with green fire.

This is indeed a wooded county. The names, the very names of the woods set a chime of memories a-ringing and these I write are only some of them, well known to me.

Great Bell Wood
Little Bell Wood
Oaken Wood
Evening Wood
Heron Wood
Wish Wood

Apr. 16th.
The Daffodils are fading fast and Herrick's words came to me as I walked. *"Fair Daffodils, we weep to see you haste away so soon..."*

There are none left in Beckley Woods, lots of blue, green foliage but the flowers are all gone for this year. The days are lengthening fast and the countryside is looking wonderful. So very green and English.

Anemones, violets, primroses, celandines and cowslip carpet the fields, woods and Downs.

Apr. 25th.
This evening I went to the Fir Wood or what remains of it, for it is fast being felled. I left the narrow track that runs through the middle and plunged into the bluebells and ferns, hating to tread on any of them - but wishing to find a quick way to the little brook which lies deep down with steep banks. I followed it to the old rustic bridge and pool. The ferns were wonderful, a finer, prettier variety than usual. Oh what a picture. I am speaking not of bracken but lovely Ferns.

Fortunately very few people seem to know this spot. I heard a cuckoo sing as I walked up the hill towards home, it was getting towards Dusk as I crossed the lane and entered my gate.

May 5th.
It's Bluebell time again. Down long vistas, the Hyacinths are like a mist or a sea of mystic blue, which to gaze at almost takes one's breath away.

To say the woods are carpeted with bluebells gives but one side of the truth. Away in the distance 'tis a flood of pale amethyst to most Royal Purple - seen near at hand. Down in Mill Wood, young winged bracken is starting up here and there in a sea of hyacinth blue. But in Beckley Wood, Rose Campions are making blots and splashes of pink and carmine among the bluebells. Each wood seems to choose its own flower trimmings in Bluebell time. In Wish Wood it is white stitchwort or as we children called them "Stars of Bethlehem". Looking at the wonder of the Bluebells - it comes to my foolish mind that they are let down from Paradise once, in the space of a year, just to remind us with a swift passing vision of the ineffable, invisible beauty beyond.

May 18th.
Today I walked to the Big Woods on the outskirts of the village with my straw basket and followed a path which I had not frequented before. This led me up, up, to where woodcutters had been working. I filled my basket with the chips of Ash, Oak and Walnut (which I wanted for my garden).

The view over Kent and Sussex was lovely - the hills of the Wittersham Ridge and the Rother Valley between and little farmhouses with their oasthouses nestling amongst trees on the edge of the Marshes. Then I followed a path that the woodcutters had made until I reached the trees again.

I wished I had gone there before the bluebells were over. They must have been wonderful, the ground was a mass of withered and seeding flower-heads.

Away the little path led me, winding here and there, till I wondered when and where I should come out into the daylight. Very dim and cool it was, in there, in the shadows. After some considerable time I found I had crossed the hill and come down into Kitchenour Lane.

May 23rd.
I went into Rye today by bus and really loved it. I had tea, brown bread and butter and three cakes in a homely Baker's upstairs room, by the Landgate.

Then I walked up to the church. It was sweet and beautiful with Whitsuntide flowers. There were only two other people in there and the solitude was welcome. So much to see and cherish in undisturbed peace!

May 26th.
This evening I knelt at my bedroom window under the thatch and took count of all the flowers in the garden.

Iris, forget-me-nots, velvety wallflowers, pinks, stocks and lilies. The paeony buds are opening and even a great scarlet poppy has burst its bonds.

Apple-blossom and cherry blossom make a drift of petals over the violet bed.

In the garish light of day the colours are almost too bright but in the dusk they gain a new quality and I felt a joy within me to see such beauty unfolding before me.

Nelly and her beloved dog in the garden of Roselands Cottage

CHAPTER TEN

SUMMER LILAC.

Jun. 1st.
The lilac is blooming again. I always feel it is something to live for each year and mine is really so very beautiful. It is called Persian Lilac.

I have read that no ghosts walk in a garden where lilac grows. What a lovely thought but I would imagine that they would come back just to smell the lilac and see it under the moon on a warm Summer's night.

Jun. 12th.
I walked in the field behind the little house this morning and picked a bunch of big pink clovers. (Their ancient name is melilot and they are said to banish sorrow.) What a delight they are. I love them for their plump homely pinkness and sweetness and I am never afraid to pick them as with more delicate flowers, Truly they have always banished sorrow. They bring me joy when I see them blooming, as they are now, with buttercups and daisies. I trod the little field paths today amidst jewelled grasses and rejoiced and I thought of Geoffrey Chaucer and repeated to myself his praise of Daisies:

> *"Then love I most those flowers white and red*
> *called Daisies.*
> *To them have I so great affection*
> *Their blissful sight softeneth all my sorrow".*

I often wonder what manner of man Chaucer was - but of one thing I feel very sure. True Knight and lover of course - but what a companion as well!

Yes I found myself repeating his words aloud, as I paced through the buttercups and daisies, till came the remembrance (maybe too late) that I might be taken for a lunatic by someone on the further side of the hedge!

Jun. 27th.
I went to visit friends in Appledore today. I walked back here from Iden (where I always leave the bus). Iden is very lovely. I have a very warm corner in my heart for it. The name always reminds me of long-ago days - long, long past. I-den like an echo - oh it is a dear spot. I have been told more than once that it is a very friendly, united little Village. Peace breathes there, it seemed to me when I was walking through it this evening. Back to Rye Foreign I went and then on to the Peasmarsh Road, up hill and down. I was a weary pilgrim by the time I reached home.

Jul. 1st.
Today I sought the Blacksmith's wife in her garden, down in the Village. Her cottage is hidden away behind the Village Street. We spoke about Rosemary to each other. I noticed that she had it growing each side of her front door and trained up against the cottage walls, yet she had not heard of the old saying, "plant Rosemary by your door and you'll never lack friends". She talked very beautifully about the virtues of the plant. She said, "it's wonderful for many things. If you have any sickly plants, plant Rosemary by them and soon they'll flourish".

She is such a pleasant woman, tall, dark and serene with a kind heart. She told me too, about the Road of

Remembrance at Folkestone; the road down which all the Soldiers had passed on their way to France. Now Rosemary has been planted along it.

Jul. 12th.
A Gypsy cart passed me in the Village Street as I walked to post a letter. The night was black dark - although the stars were out. I felt a little afraid as the light from my torch was weak with a small beam.

I suddenly heard a cart very near and I got onto the raised side of the Lane. I felt my arm grasped and saw a Gypsy man who said, "don't be afraid Lady, I'll not run you over". It was startling but I felt sure he meant me no harm. I like the Gypsies. I have a fellow-feeling for them. It's their homelessness I expect and the moving on, as my life has been for the past few years. Yes, I feel a kindred spirit with them.

Jul. 20th.
I took a bus to Winchelsea today. What a dream it all is, all green peace. The main road is wonderful with great over-arching trees and so wide. They call it the Monk's Walk. What romantic place.

The people who dwell there really take care of it. Many of them must be very wealthy as much money has been spent on the church, "The Dear Church", which stands in the centre of this little town. I was told it is to have some new windows which are to be like the beautiful original ones. I read in an old book that those windows were of mellow colours and their affect on the noble architecture was to produce an air of mystery, a mystic sense of Holy presence abiding within its walls.

Aug. 1st.
Today Doris and Roddy came unexpectedly and they took me for a drive to Hartfield and then Withyham where we had tea in an ancient farmhouse which has been turned into an Inn called the Dorset Arms. We went out in the garden before leaving - such a lovely, old-world garden with flowers everywhere and a duckpond with an orchard behind an old flint wall. We walked up hill though fields to visit the church - which is very beautifully situated on top of the hill above the small village. Great trees surround the little churchyard in which masses of wild flowers are growing.

In a great side chapel of the church is one of the most striking, life-like groups of figure that I have ever seen, around the tomb of a little lad of thirteen years - the thirteenth child of the Earl of Dorset and his countess (1600). The child rests half recumbent on the top of the sarcophagus, his small face looking upward into space. He leans on one elbow, in his other arm, half concealed, is a skull. His mother, full of sorrow, kneels beside him gazing earnestly into his face, her head supported by a beautifully moulded hand and arm. On the other side of the tomb kneels his Father, his face marvellously rendered. You notice at once how like the frail boy's face is, to that of his manly father. The air of dignity and character is impossible to describe and the look of fathomless sorrow. I could have lingered there for hours beside that wonderful tomb and studied the glorious stained window above it which portrays all the coats of arms and their quarterings with names of the Dorset family long ago.

We had a pleasant drive back to Peasmarsh through wooded country and pretty villages.

Aug. 20th.
As I write the grey light of Dawn is growing rosy, bringing with it the promise of another glorious day. We have had a week of truly wonderful weather - a real bit of old-fashioned summer!

Yesterday I went to Ashford by bus. It is quite a long journey and the bus was packed. I was very hot by the time we reached the town, in fact my face was flaming with heat!

It really is a dear, pleasant, old town. Not a bit as I have always pictured it and the surrounding hilly country very pretty. The River Stour wanders through Ashford and I found a picturesque corner where it flowed under a bridge among the flour mills and I longed to linger. The streets slope and you get views of the hills beyond.

A magnificent old church stands near the town centre with some interesting tombs of the Smythe family, (1500-1600) in a wonderful state of preservation. The Smythes were *the* great people of Ashford in those days - Landowners and now that I have seen their wonderful tombs I shall always have respect for Smythes! There was an Irish Title too, belonging to them; they were Earls and Grandees of Portugal and they had intermarried with the Sydneys. I think this particular branch is extinct.

I must go to Ashford again, if only to hear once more the singularly lovely music of the bells of Ashford Church. Very mellow, soft and sweet, making a strange, penetrating, resonant music through the busy sounds and noises of the busy, crowded High Street.

Aug. 31st.
I left home early and walked to the Hill. On the way up, I saw the loveliest field of wild-flowers, growing rampant and so big and fine of colour, all sorts of flowers in masses, bigger and stronger than their struggling sisters of the road-side. I fancy they must have looked just the same to the ancient Britons.

There were many Robins about. How absurdly cocky and dear they are. Bindweed and elderflower are growing profusely in the hedges and there is still honeysuckle in places.

When I reached the top of the hill I sank down into the grass and drank in the view.

Sep. 6th.
Harvest in is full swing. Every day I see great wains going home loaded along the little lanes.

The apples are ripening on my orchard trees so I must prepare the apple room for them. (This is a little brick building which stands in a corner of my garden near the hedge. It has a stone floor and is quite roomy and pleasant inside.)

The turnips I planted in the garden are doing wonderfully well; I gave Mrs. Crittal (a neighbour) a nice lot last Saturday, all scrubbed snow white. She returned my plate today with three most lovely sweet-smelling Roses.

My Scarlet Runners and Marrows are nearly ready for picking. What a delight it is to be able to eat fresh, home-grown vegetables.

Sep. 9th.
So far we are having a very beautiful September. I just returned from a walk with Nellie over the fields to the South.

The pure white cups of the bindweed and a few, very few yellow and purple, shaggy and faded flowers are still to be seen and the hedges are bearing Blackberries, Sloes and Nuts.

The air was so lovely, so soft and scented.

Bracken is turning gold and great vistas of it carpet the woods: a lovely sight with the late evening sun lighting up the glades. The trees still have most of their leaves. I met not a soul nor heard any voices except for the moo of a cow from a nearby pasture. I got home in the deep dusk when the bats were flying.

Sep. 15th.
A friend drove me to Fairlight today - we took a picnic lunch. We walked down into the Glen to the Dripping Well and followed the little rushing stream down in the beautiful glen almost to where it falls into the sea. it was certainly lovely there.

CHAPTER ELEVEN
WEALDEN HOLIDAY.

Sep. 30th.
Today Roddie drove Nell and me to Mayfield to stay with dear Mrs. Weston for two weeks. Mayfield is a Wealden Village which is situated on a ridge between Ashdown Forest and Heathfield. The cottage I am staying in is very old and pretty in East Street.

After supper I took the dog for a run and went up the Village Street to the top of Fletching Street. The stars shone out, the sky was a tender night blue and the Moon lighted up the spaces between the ancient houses - those great spaces looking Southward with the faint line of hills in the distance Heathfield way.

The air was perfectly still - the little shop windows were sparkling with light, so bright and the dear old Village Street fell away into the dimness with the clear-cut silhouette of its antique roofs and chimneys against the clear sky.

Oct. 3rd.
As I write the Village bells are chiming, or rather, pealing out. It is a calm, fine night. I went for an absolutely lovely walk this afternoon. Mrs. Weston went with me and the dog.

First we walked to Argos Hill, climbed to the top and then down the Western side into a warm, sunny valley out of the cold wind. We walked past woods and all sorts of quaint cottages until, at last, we had completed three sides of a circle and found ourselves under a signpost which said '2 miles to Mayfield' and then we took the road which goes by the barracks (as they call the old, haunted houses) and Rotherdale. I cannot describe in words good enough, the gorgeous colouring of the countryside as I saw it today, all backed up by blue distance, miles and miles of the lovely, hilly, wooded countryside wherever I looked; in short the Sussex Weald. It was exquisite. On all sides the Weald lay dreaming in a soft Autumn haze.

Oct. 6th.

Yesterday I found a bridle path behind a picturesque farm. I found it wound on and on between two high hedges and little woods without a sign of life but for the wind rustling in the dry beech leaves. I got just a little bit nervous there because I felt I might never be found again if I sprained my ankle or fell! Besides, I wasn't sure where it led to. The mud was unspeakable in places but by moving quickly I didn't sink.

At last I came out on the top of a hill and those high hedges were with me all the way. I enjoyed nutting in a little copse. I scrambled up and down all sorts of rough places to reach the biggest clusters. I followed a little stream through a wood. I then heard the creaking of a windmill and found myself on Argos Hill. I looked South towards Mayfield and the Downs. Mayfield seemed so low down but even from that distance I could see the church.

There is a singularly beautiful view of the church from the bottom of the ridge on which Mayfield stands.

Looking upwards, one sees it high above, embosomed in trees, lovely and soothing in its protecting peacefulness.

Oct. 8th.
I have just returned from a long walk with Nell down Rotherdale. I turned off at the pathway and went up the hill past the old farmhouse which stands alone with two ponds, one quite a large one with ornamental grass growing in clumps along its further shore. It seemed very lonely there. I found some BIG blackberries on a bush beside the path - huge ones! In another spot white Michaelmas Daisies and perennial Sunflowers were growing.

I left the pathway and went though a little white gate leading into a winding lane which was bordered by Yew trees, all well clipped and so high and ancient. I wondered how many centuries they had stood there. Further on I passed another farm, very picturesque and colourful with its hay stacks, old barns and green setting. Then I went down the hill and the air grew softer and warmer as I neared the village.

Oct. 9th.
This afternoon I walked to Tidebrook, it is so pretty there. Perched up above the village is the lovely old Manor House.

I went to the church and found a children's service taking place. I heard fragments of the beautiful address being given to the Tidebrook children as I sat in the old church porch and I glimpsed a fine profile and white surplice. I was eager to see the whole person with the clear voice and fluent, happy speech and the outstanding sincerity - so I waited and when at last he appeared I found him to be quite young with clear grey eyes and a kind face.

Lucky little Tidebrook to be taught about the Scriptures by such a Vicar in such a spot in dear England. Oh, thank God for such men.

Oct. 10th.
I have just come back from an evening walk down Fletching Street with Nellie. I picked blackberries on a hedge where the little Rother sings and murmurs and ripples its way under the bridge and past Mrs. Kent's garden. All the little Sussex rivers and streams are roaring along in their rocky beds since a heavy rainfall earlier today. I am so enjoying my holiday. Dear Mrs. Weston has looked after me so well. She is such a kind, thoughtful person.

Oct. 12th.
Yesterday Mrs. Weston and I caught the 9.30 a.m. train from Mayfield to Eastbourne. It was a fine, calm day and the sun shone.

When we crossed the Heathfield Ridge the country became quite flat and uninteresting - even the people seemed different - oh give me the forest ridge! Then we saw the beginning of the Downs, with the red brick of the Eastbourne Suburbs, like a waste of sharp-pointed brick-bats, with here and there an advance guard creeping up into the remoteness beyond.

We changed trains at Eastbourne and reached our destination, Pevensey, in due course. All I wanted was the sea and while Mrs. Weston enquired about return trains, I turned my back on Pevensey and Westham to where, across the Marshes, I saw a line of Martello Towers.

We took a hard, high, road that appeared to lead there and walked for ages until at last we reached the beach,

rather a desolate, ugly piece of coast where a particularly nasty murder was committed some years ago. We walked along the beach until we arrived in Pevensey bay, where we lunched in a little hotel overlooking the sea.
After our meal we walked back to Pevensey, so old - and sleepy. The church in Westham is one of the oldest in that part of Sussex, Norman and very beautiful. Pevensey Church is smaller and almost wholly of the 13th Century.

We went over the Old Mint House which I found *most* interesting. It reminded me of the Old House, Middle Street, Deal. It is very large with about twenty-eight rooms full of lovely things, and a ghost.

We did not have time to go over the castle but we saw it as we walked through its grounds within the huge Roman walls. We had tea in Westham before catching our train to Eastbourne. We spent an hour there - walked down the fine main street with its most attractive shops, to the Sea Front. It was nearly dark by this time and we stood on the front and looked out to sea.

We were weary and ready for our beds by the time we reached Mayfield.

Oct. 13th.
I have become a "Stool Ball" Fan! I have been watching matches and practices here. Today Mrs. Weston and I went by bus to Tunbridge Wells to watch the County Match between women and girls of Sussex and Kent.

It was a lovely drive through Frant and Mark Cross - all woodlands and views over the Weald and Crowborough Beacon, right away to the North Downs in Surrey and Kent. Ten pence return - so it was not expensive for such a nice drive.

I thoroughly enjoyed the match. I'm afraid that Kent were far beyond Sussex in style. We sat looking on for some hours, even in the rain, but when it came down in torrents, we departed. The match was held on the County Cricket Ground, high up on the Common. No doubt Kent won. So brave Kent, say I. (My heart, for many years, has been torn between those two charmers - Kent and Sussex.)

We had tea in a café in the beautiful Pantiles before catching our bus back to Mayfield.

Oct. 14th.
Roddy and Doris fetched me at 11 o'clock and after coffee with Mrs. Weston we departed for Peasmarsh.

It was a golden Autumn day as we drove through Wealden villages. We stopped at Hawkhurst for lunch at an old Inn which is associated with the Hawkhurst Smuggling Gang.

What a lovely holiday I have had and so many beautiful place visited - dear and pleasant memories to look back upon.

CHAPTER TWELVE
RETURN TO PEASMARSH.

Oct. 20th.
I found three precious little violets and a wild rose on my walk today along the Wittersham Road. The woods are still golden with bracken and the beech trees still hold on to their shining copper leaves.

It was getting near dusk as I neared home and through the tree branches I saw the quiet evening sky in pale colour and the stars appearing. It was a bewitching picture. Then and there I wanted to paint it!

Oct. 31st. Peasmarsh.
You cannot imagine how *glorious* the weather is and so nice and dry underfoot, that I can walk for miles. It is like summer and actually here and there are wild roses on the hedge, not like the ordinary pearl-pink ones we see in June but that charming little white rose, sometimes a whole cluster on one stem, more like a white rambler but single - I think it is called "the Burnet Rose". It seems strange to see Roses and Holly growing together.

Nov. 10th.
I went for what seemed a long walk this afternoon - only *seemed* because when I came to a signpost it informed me that I was but one and a quarter miles from Peasmarsh!

The weather so far this month has been dreary but not too cold. The country is tucked up for its Winter sleep and rest. The hedgerows are aglow with Holly, Hips and Haws - such a wealth of crimson to brighten these days and a plentiful supply of food for the birds.

Nov. 12th.
What a comfort Nellie is to me, my sole companion in my cottage home. To know she is there when I return from shopping, and to talk to her and to take her on my walks. What would I do without her?

I often think of dear Peter who was in Canada with me. I can almost feel the silky touch of that beautiful, noble head as he laid his head on my lap waiting for me to stroke him. If I was slow to do so, he would thrust his nose under my hand to remind me he was waiting to be stroked.

I had a dream the other night about a dark passage and a dog coming towards me, head bent near the ground as if eagerly tracing a loved presence. This passage must be the "Dogs' Passage" where they come and go to meet us and find us. O Dogs, precious companions, dearer than any human friends. There is a bit in Mark Twain about the dog which is led in the funeral processions of the Parsees in India. He said the reason that a dog led, arose from a Persian belief that the dog led souls to Heaven. What a lovely thought.

Nov. 15th.
Today I made my Christmas Puddings, with doors and windows wide open! The farm cock was crowing and sun-shine flooded the old kitchen while the fire burned merrily.

I spread the table with clean white pantry paper and then weighed the flour and suet and prepared the bread-crumbs; washed the dried fruit and then mixed all the ingredients and wished as I stirred.

It is evening now and the puddings are boiling happily on the range. As I write the dog is asleep beside me. I have a flickering candle in a brass candlestick on my knee with an inkbottle on the arm of my chair. If an earthquake comes I will be sprinkled with candle-grease and ink!

Dec. 1st.
While I slept a miracle took place. Today the countryside is covered with a blanket of snow. Every blade of grass and plant lies sleeping beneath it. The trees look magical with their snow covered branches glistening in the sun. There is a deep blue sky and everywhere looks like a fairy land.

Dec. 2nd.
We are snowed in and this is no exaggeration. Great drifts which make roads in and out of Peasmarsh impassable; no Postman or Baker today. My telephone still works. (I'm hoping that the weight of the snow does not break the lines.) It is still snowing as I write and I've spent the day cosily in the cottage beside a roaring log fire.

Dec. 18th.
I walked over the frozen lanes a long way today to the church. The nice old toothless Sexton was working in the churchyard amongst the tombs. Many had little Holly wreaths upon them.

The church was looking lovely and *Christmas-y*, decorated with boughs of fir and holly with a delightful crib near the altar. I sat for a while relishing the peace and beauty of this ancient place.

Dec. 18th.
Tonight carol singers came with their flickering lanterns and joyous voices. How beautifully the sang "Silent Night". It reminded me of the Christmases I'd spent in Southern Germany when I was young.

I invited them in for mince-pies and cocoa and they warmed themselves beside my fire before setting off up the frosty, moonlit lane. I stood at my door listening to their voices until they could be heard no more.

Christmas Eve.
Roddy arrived last night and this morning helped me decorate the cottage. We have hung bunches of holly and mistletoe in the hall. We have a lovely fir-tree in the sitting room which we hung with my old German decorations bought when I was a girl in Karlsruhe.

I have made a centre piece for the Dining Room Table from Traveller's Joy (Wild Clematis) and Holly, nuts, oranges and apples. Nellie looks very pretty with a big scarlet bow attached to her collar.

I have just finished stuffing a small Turkey which Roddy bought at Selfridges (£1.1s.9d.). We will have baked potatoes and parsnips, sprouts and bread sauce with it and one of my Christmas puddings to follow. My stuffing recipe consists of sausagemeat, suet, breadcrumbs, herbs, lemon rind and an egg to bind it together.

Tonight the trees are outlined against a dark blue, frosty sky with the moon like a great gold coin shining down on my garden.

Christmas Day.
I woke as dawn was breaking and watched the sunrise from my bed. My thoughts took me back to other Christmases: my childhood ones at my Grandparents' home, The Royal Hotel, Deal, when all the family gathered together; my teenage ones in Southern Germany; my early married ones in Canada (where I was homesick and cold) and later ones after Winnie and Roddy were born.

After breakfast Roddy drove me to the church, where we attended matins and heard the lovely story of that first Christmas and sang Carols.

We dined by candlelight and toasted absent loved ones across the sea. Afterwards we sat by the fire and reminisced.

Dec. 31st.
Another year has passed and here I am sitting by my bedroom window looking out upon the moonlit garden. It is nearly midnight and soon a New Year will start and I must move on to a new abode. I have truly enjoyed my time here and will always remember this cottage with warm affection.

Does every beautiful thing and memory that my heart bids farewell to here, wing its way upwards to form part of a dwelling place beyond the stars?